IMAGES OF WAR

THE CRIMEAN WAR

RARE PHOTOGRAPHS FROM WARTIME ARCHIVES

John Grehan and Martin Mace

Pen & Sword
MILITARY

First published in Great Britain in 2013 by
PEN & SWORD MILITARY
An imprint of
Pen & Sword Books Ltd
47 Church Street
Barnsley
South Yorkshire
S70 2AS

ISBN 978-1-78159-383-7

Typeset by Concept, Huddersfield, West Yorkshire HD4 5JL.
Printed and bound in England by CPI Group (UK) Ltd, Croydon CR0 4YY.

Pen & Sword Books Ltd incorporates the imprints of Pen & Sword Archaeology, Atlas, Aviation, Battleground, Discovery, Family History, History, Maritime, Military, Naval, Politics, Railways, Select, Social History, Transport, True Crime, and Claymore Press, Frontline Books, Leo Cooper, Praetorian Press, Remember When, Seaforth Publishing and Wharncliffe.

For a complete list of Pen & Sword titles please contact
PEN & SWORD BOOKS LIMITED
47 Church Street, Barnsley, South Yorkshire, S70 2AS, England
E-mail: enquiries@pen-and-sword.co.uk
Website: www.pen-and-sword.co.uk

Contents

Acknowledgements

All images courtesy of the US Library of Congress and other public domain sources, except where specified.

4

Introduction

'Lord Raglan wishes the cavalry to advance rapidly to the front, and try to prevent the enemy carrying away the guns. Troop of horse-artillery may accompany. French cavalry is on your left. Immediate. (Signed) R. Airey'.

These few words set in motion the most famous cavalry action in British military history – the Charge of the Light Brigade. The charge took place at the Battle of Balaklava, an engagement which exemplified the nature of the war conducted in the Crimea. The charge with sabre and lance, with cold steel, was little different from that delivered by British cavalry at Waterloo forty years earlier or even a century earlier at Dettingen. Yet, also at Balaklava, one of the most famous infantry actions took place which heralded a new era in warfare.

A single battalion of infantry, the 93rd (Highland) Regiment, the Sutherland Highlanders, was all that stood between 2,500 Russian cavalry and the British camp. Faced with such a force of cavalry an infantry battalion would normally form square. However, Major General Sir Colin Campbell's men had recently cast aside their smoothbore muskets in favour of Minié rifles and they no longer feared the cavalry. The difference between the two types of weapon was enormous. The effective range of the smoothbore was considered to be little more than 100 to 150 yards; that of the rifle was about 600 yards. Its accuracy can be gauged by the quoted statistics that at the Battle of Vitoria in 1813 it required the expenditure of 459 bullets to hit one man, whereas at the battles of Alma and Inkerman one bullet in sixteen found its mark.

The result of this development in weapons technology was that Campbell's 'Thin Red Line' stood its ground and its long-range, accurate volleys stopped the Russian cavalry in its tracks. In the space of just over a minute the tactics of the old order had been blown away, and a new phrase had entered the English lexicon.

The trench warfare, and the terrible conditions the men had to endure for almost a year in front of Sevastopol, were in essence the same as those experienced by a later generation at Ypres or on the Somme, as were the great artillery bombardments that preceded each major assault upon the city. Yet this was the middle of the nineteenth century and khaki battledress and steel helmets had yet to replace red tunics and bearskins.

This juxtaposition between the old and the new was also evident at sea. The Crimean War brought into action the three largest battle fleets in the world at that time. The British and French had begun to replace the sailing ships of old for the steam-driven paddle or screw-propelled warships. The French even deployed armoured floating batteries in the latter stages of the war. Both Allied navies though still relied very heavily on sailing ships, and steam and sail could be seen together crossing the waters of the Black Sea. Russia had also started to introduce steam ships into its service but was considerably behind its enemies.

Another innovation which influenced the war, albeit indirectly, was the introduction of the telegraph. For the first time messages could be sent back from the battlefield to the UK with unprecedented speed. This allowed the first war correspondent (another new development) William Russell of *The Times* to submit his reports shortly after the actions they described. The British public soon learnt of the bravery of its troops and a murmur rapidly became an outcry demanding recognition for the ordinary soldiers. The result was the introduction of the Victoria Cross. The effect of such an award was considered to be the equivalent of reinforcing the army in the Crimea. 'The value attached by soldiers to a little bit of ribbon,' argued the Duke of Newcastle, the Secretary of State for War, somewhat condescendingly, 'is such as to render any danger insignificant and any privation light if it can be attained.' The medal would also, according to Newcastle, bring in more recruits than any other measure that had hitherto been adopted.

The other technological advance for which the Crimean War has become renowned was the camera. It was only in 1836 that the first practical camera had been invented and the Crimean War became only the third conflict to be recorded, if not on film, on photo-sensitive paper – and is the reason for the publication of the book.

The first-ever images from the front were taken by a Hungarian photographer called Carol Popp de Szathmari. He recorded images from the American-Mexican War of 1846–1847 and took his camera into the Danube provinces in 1853 when the Crimean War first broke out. The more extensive and more widely-known are the photographs by Roger Fenton. Commissioned by the Manchester publisher Thomas Agnew, and officially recognised by the British Government, Roger Fenton arrived at Balaklava on the Black Sea on 8 March 1855. He was not actually the first photographer sent out to the Crimea. He was a replacement for Richard Nicklin who, along with his assistants – two Royal Engineers – equipment and invaluable photographs, was lost when their ship, *Rip Van Winkle*, sank during a hurricane that struck Balaklava harbour on 14 November 1854. The Engineers were replaced by two more, Ensigns Brandon and Dawson, who reached the Crimea in the spring of 1855. Exactly how many photographs they took remains undetermined as they were all retained by the Army and never publically displayed. The photos were not cared for and by 1869 they were in very poor condition and have now been lost altogether.

Something old, something new. Side by side in Balaklava harbour lie a steam-driven warship (on the right of the picture) and a number of older traditional Royal Navy sailing ships. Of the eighty-four British ships that operated in the Black Sea throughout the course of the Crimean War, just thirteen were old sailing vessels, the rest were either screw propulsion or paddle-driven. In the main it was the sailing ships that carried the heaviest weaponry, though the screw-propelled HMS *Royal Albert* carried the most guns, with 121. The French fleet of thirty-eight ships had sixteen sailing warships.

Fenton's photographs, on the other hand, have, in the main, been well-preserved. In the three months or so he spent in the Crimea (until 26 June 1855) Fenton produced 360 photographs of which many copies survive.

When Fenton left the Crimea, James Robertson, the chief engraver of the Imperial Mint at Constantinople, and an enthusiastic amateur photographer, travelled to the Crimea. His photographs act, effectively, as a continuation of Fenton's work, though Robertson was not acting in an official capacity. Another amateur photographer that arrived at Balaklava in 1855 was George Shaw Lefevre. Twelve of his photos were published at his own expense in April 1856. A retired French Army Colonel, Jean-Charles Langlois also sailed to the Crimea along with Léon-Eugène Méhédin. Together they took a number of excellent photographs which were later displayed in Paris in 1860. Images from all of these photographers are included in this book.

Fenton could not photograph the Charge of the Light Brigade, which had taken place the previous October, but he did take a picture of the 'valley of death' which was still littered with the cannon balls fired at the light dragoons, lancers and hussars that comprised the Six Hundred immortalised in Tennyson's verse. It is one of the photographs presented in this book, though there is considerable controversy surrounding this photograph, with many claiming that it was 'staged', and that it is not the ground over which the Light Brigade charged.

As for the Light Brigade, it carried out Lord Raglan's orders to move against the Russian guns. Unfortunately it was the wrong guns. Nevertheless Cardigan led his men into the valley of death for, as we know, it was not theirs to question why. As Maréchal Bosquet, watching the drama unfold, observed, 'It is magnificent, but it is not war.' Maybe the meaning of his words has been misinterpreted. Possibly what he really said was, 'It is magnificent, but it is no longer war as we know it'?

Chapter One

The Commanders and Their Staff

Many and varied are the pretexts for war. An archduke can be assassinated in a distant Balkan province, a king can lose his head to the Paris mob, or a cargo of tea can be dumped in an American harbour. The pretext for the Crimean War was possession of a bunch of keys.

The keys in question were those to the Church and Grotto of the Nativity in Bethlehem. Their ownership was disputed by Catholic and Orthodox monks, and this pitted Tsar Nicholas I of Russia, the defender of the Orthodox Church in the East, against France, the protector of the Latin Church. This clash of wills soon led to a clash of arms.

Of course the real reason why war broke out in 1853 had nothing to do with a few litigious monks. The Holy Land formed part of the Turkish Ottoman Empire and the theological dispute enabled Nicholas to intervene in Turkish affairs. The Tsar sought access to the Mediterranean for his Black Sea fleet and Turkey, whom the Tsar labelled 'the sick man of Europe', stood in his way.

France and Britain had no intention of allowing Russian warships to enter the eastern Mediterranean and when Russia and Turkey finally came to blows, the two Western powers combined to send an expeditionary force to defend Constantinople. As it transpired, the sick man staged a remarkable recovery and the Russian invasion of Turkey's Danube provinces was repulsed. There was really no longer any military justification for the continuation of the Allied expedition. But war is often harder to stop than to start. Napoleon III longed for a victory to solidify his position as France's Emperor, and in Britain the Press urged the Government to seize Sevastopol, the Black Sea Fleet's main base in the Crimea.

Though the war with Russia was conducted in the Caucasus, the Baltic, the White Sea, the Far East and the Pacific, it was the expedition to the Crimea which became the main focus of the Allied Powers. Thus the 'Russian War' became known as the Crimean War.

* * *

The French element of the expeditionary force assembled by the Allies (known as *l'Armée d'Orient*) was divided into four divisions, with two brigades of cavalry; that of the British was five infantry divisions, one of which was a Light Division, and a Cavalry Division. By the end of May 1854, the bulk of this combined force had reached Turkey, encamped at Scutari opposite Constantinople, to wait upon developments.

(*Facing page*) The Commander-in-Chief of the British force was the 66-year-old General FitzRoy James Henry Somerset, 1st Baron Raglan. Lord Raglan was a highly experienced soldier, his career having begun in 1804 when he was commissioned into the 4th Light Dragoons, later joining the staff of Sir Arthur Wellesley, the future Duke of Wellington, at the Battle of Copenhagen. He continued to serve with Wellesley throughout the Peninsular War as his principle aide-de-camp and then his Military Secretary. He also fought with Wellington in the Waterloo campaign where he was severely wounded, losing his right hand. When Wellington became Commander-in-Chief of the Army, Somerset continued as his Military Secretary. In 1854 he was promoted to full General and given command of the Eastern Army. Raglan became a Field Marshal following the Battle of Inkerman in November 1855. On 29 June 1855 he died due to complications brought on by a bout of dysentery. Though well-liked by some, Raglan proved to be indecisive and his orders inexplicit, as exemplified by his instructions to the Light Brigade at Balaklava. According to one Guards officer, Colonel Henry Percy, Raglan, 'never shows himself not even after an action, to the men ... [he] has thrown away his opportunities of being known to the troops, he is a myth to half of them'. Fanny Duberly gave this assessment of Raglan following his death: 'We are almost tempted to lose sight of the inefficient General, in the recollection of the kind-hearted, gentlemanly man, who had so hard a task, which he fulfilled so well, of keeping together and in check the heads of so many armies.'

This photograph shows Lord Raglan's Headquarters, with Lord Raglan, Marshal Pélissier, Lord Burghersh and an Aide-de-camp of Marshal Pélissier. The man second to the right is listed by Fenton as a 'Spahi'. What he meant was Sipahi. These were professional Turkish cavalry, some of which formed the household mounted troops of the Ottoman Palace.

Raglan's Adjutant-General was Sir James Estcourt. In his thirty-four years of service in the Army, James Bucknall Bucknall Estcourt had never seen action, yet on 21 February 1854 he was made a Brigadier-General and was appointed Adjutant-General to the expeditionary force in the Crimea. He was regarded as being quite incapable of fulfilling his new role and it is said that Raglan did not even 'pay him the compliment of attempting to transact business with him'. Nevertheless, he was a friend of Raglan and he was promoted to Major-General on 12 December 1854. It soon became apparent that Estcourt was out of his depth and the Secretary of State for War, the Duke of Newcastle, demanded that both Estcourt and Richard Airey (see below) should be recalled. Estcourt, however, was struck down by cholera during the siege of Sevastopol and he died on the morning of 24 June 1855.

As a young officer with the 1st Regiment of Foot Guards (later the Grenadier Guards) Sir James Simpson served in the Peninsular War and the Waterloo campaign. He later commanded the 29th Regiment in Mauritius and India. In February 1855, as a full General, he was sent out to the Crimea to act as Raglan's chief of staff. When Raglan died in June, Simpson reluctantly took command of the army in the Crimea. He resigned that post on 10 November, 'mortified and disgusted' at his treatment in the British press, which continuously criticized his handling of the army. 'He deserves recall,' ran *The Times* after the British failure to capture the Sevastopol Redan on 8 September 1855. 'The British army had been beaten, and beaten, it was reasonable to suppose, through the incapacity of the General ... It cannot be too often that our army requires a younger man ... not [a man] of the age of the British Commander-in-Chief who sits in a ditch muffled up in a cloak when a whole army rushes to the assault'. Command of the army devolved upon William Codrington.

Though he was the son of an admiral, General Sir William John Codrington GCB, chose a career in the Army, joining the 88th Regiment in 1821. In September 1854 he was appointed to the command of the 1st Brigade of the Light Division. Codrington took command of the division after Sir George Brown was wounded. After the resignation of General James Simpson in November 1855, though still only a substantive major-general, he became Commander-in-Chief of the British Army in the Crimea. So the man that had set off for the Crimea as a regimental major ended the war as a Lieutenant General. Codrington owed his promotion, according to Captain Earle, to being part of the influential 'Guards set' in the Crimea, 'and their influence built the nest which is now filled with their protégés'.

Sir John Burgoyne had a highly distinguished career, though this was tarnished somewhat during the Crimean War. He served in the Peninsular War and in the American war of 1812. In 1838, he became a Major General and in 1845 was named Inspector-General of Fortifications, the executive head of the Royal Engineers. He was appointed Raglan's Chief Engineer for the Crimean War, though he had been opposed to the expedition in the first place, having been sent out ahead to consider the practicalities of the operation. In his report he wrote: 'No operation is of such doubtful issue as the landing in an enemy's country for the purpose of conquest.' Whilst he later opposed a quick assault upon Sevastopol because it would result in too many casualties, he had earlier declared that 'it can have little strength as a fortress'. He was recalled to the UK due to the lack of progress in the siege (Colonel Henry Percy VC called him an 'inefficient old twaddle'). Nevertheless, he retired in 1868 as a Field Marshal.

Lieutenant General Sir John Campbell shown here (sitting) with Captain Hume his aide-de-camp. Sir John Campbell entered the army as an Ensign in the 38th regiment in 1821. He rose through the ranks being promoted to the rank of Colonel by brevet on 11 November 1851. The Crimean War offered the chance of further promotion and he was given the 2nd Brigade of Sir Richard England's 3rd Division. After the Battle of Inkerman he was promoted to Major General and as the senior brigadier with the army he was given temporary command of the 4th Division following the death of Lord Cathcart. On 7 June 1855 he was superseded by Lieutenant General Lord Bentinck. For the attack upon the Redan on 18 June 1855, he volunteered to lead the storming party of the 4th Division. He was killed as he rushed out of the trenches.

This photo shows Colonel David Edward Wood, Major Stuart Wortley and Colonel the Honourable Francis Colborne which Fenton said were on the staff of Sir Richard England. Forty-six-years-old General Richard England commanded the 3rd Division at the start of the Crimean campaign. Though said by Roger Fenton that England was 'a bad general but a very good horseman', England seems to have behaved magnificently at the Battle of the Alma. His division suffered severely during the winter of 1854–5 and in August 1855 he was forced to return to the UK through illness. When he departed from the Crimea he was the last of the General officers that had left the UK in charge of a division. Colonel Wood was actually an artillery officer who commanded the artillery of the 4th Division. Later in the campaign Wood took over command of the Horse Artillery. Francis Colborne was an Assistant Quartermaster-General.

Scottish-born Lieutenant General Sir George Brown began his military career with the 43rd Regiment in 1806. He was involved in the Battle of Copenhagen in 1807 and in the Peninsular War, his battalion forming part of the famous Light Division. After serving in America Brown received a staff appointment at Horse Guards, becoming a Lieutenant General and Adjutant-General to the Forces. Brown relinquished the latter post in 1853. When the force was assembled for the Crimea, Brown was given command of the Light Division, and was nominally Raglan's second in command. Though he was said to be the most unpopular general in the army he led a successful subsidiary expedition against the port of Kertch in May 1855 to cut off supplies reaching the Russians from there. He was invalided home on 29 June 1855, the same day that Lord Raglan died. This photograph shows Brown with officers of his staff: Major Hallewell, Colonel Brownrigg, an orderly, Colonel Airey, Captain Pearson, Captain Markham, and Captain Ponsonby.

Irish-born Sir George De Lacy Evans GCB entered the British Army as a Gentleman Volunteer in 1806 and the following year he obtained an ensigncy in the 22nd Regiment. He exchanged into the 3rd Light Dragoons, in which regiment he was involved in the Peninsular War. De Lacy Evans took part in the 1812 and 1814 conflicts in America. He returned to Britain in time to fight with Wellington at Waterloo. At the age of sixty-six he was given command of the 2nd Division for the Crimean expedition. After the heavy losses at the Battle of Inkerman, and with no apparent progress in the siege of Sevastopol, De Lacy Evans urged Raglan to abandon the expedition altogether. When the Duke of Cambridge resigned (see below) so did Evans and he returned to England sick and disillusioned. Their departure sparked an exodus, and in the two months after Inkerman 225 officers left the Crimea.

Lieutenant General Pennefather started his career in the Army as a Cornet in the 7th Dragoon Guards in 1818, transferring to the 22nd Regiment of Foot with which regiment he became a Lieutenant Colonel, working his way up the officer grades without having to purchase any of his commissions. Pennefather saw active service in India and Ireland. In 1854 he was given command of the first brigade of the De Lacy Evans' division. His conduct at the Battle of Inkerman earned him much praise. On 20 June he was made Major General. Pennefather succeeded to the command of the 2nd Division when Evans returned to England in the latter part of November. He was invalided from the Crimea in July 1855. Here he is shown with his staff consisting of Captain Wing, Captain Layard, Captain Ellison, Colonel Wilbraham, Colonel Percy Herbert, Major Thackwell and Dr Wood.

Sir Colin Campbell first saw action with the 9th Regiment in the Peninsular War, where he was twice wounded. He also served in the War of 1812 and later in India, where he was wounded again. In 1854 he was given command of the Highland Brigade, which later became the Highland Division, which he led throughout the Crimean War with the rank of Major General. Campbell continued to distinguish himself during the Indian Mutiny and he eventually rose to the rank of Field Marshal. Fenton had difficulty photographing Colin Campbell as 'he is up at four every morning and either writing and not to be disturbed, or scampering about'.

Coldstream Guardsman Lieutenant General Sir Henry J.W. Bentinck, KCB, was appointed an aide-de-camp to Queen Victoria in 1841. He became a Major General in June 1854 and with that rank sailed to the Crimea in command of the Brigade of Guards. He was attached to the 4th Division after the death of Sir George Cathcart. Though he led the Guards 'most gallantly' at the Battle of Inkerman, where he was wounded, Bentinck, according to one fellow officer 'turned out to be an arrant imposter'.

Another admiral's son who became a general was Sir Charles Ash Windham (whom Fenton calls Ashe Windham). He joined the Coldstream guards at the age of sixteen and served with the regiment in Canada. He was retired on half-pay when the Crimean War broke out but, with the rank of Colonel, he was appointed to the post of Assistant Quartermaster-General of the 4th Division. Following General Cathcart's death, and wounds to other more senior officers, he succeeded to the command of the 4th Division. He distinguished himself at the storming of Sevastopol's Redan on 8 September 1855 and was promoted to the rank of Major General. When William Codrington took over command of the army Windham became his Chief-of-Staff.

General Sir Richard Airey entered the Army as an ensign of the 34th Regiment. He evidently showed a capacity for staff work as he served as an aide-de-camp to two generals before becoming an Assistant Adjutant-General at the Horse Guards and then Military Secretary to the Commander-in-Chief. Though he was given command of the 1st Brigade of the Light Division in the army in the Crimea, he was soon appointed to the post of Quartermaster-General under Raglan. Following *The Times* editorial of 23 December 1854 accusing the army's high command of 'incompetency, lethargy, aristocratic hauteur and official indifference' to the conditions of the soldiers, the Duke of Newcastle demanded that Airey be recalled. Lord Raglan, nevertheless, stood by his man and Airey retained this post under Simpson and Codrington and was made a Major General. He is shown here with Major Hallewell.

Henry William Barnard joined the Grenadier Guards in 1814. By the time of the expedition to the Crimea Barnard was a Major General. He was given command of a brigade in Sir Richard England's division. After Lord Raglan's death Barnard became General Simpson's chief-of-staff, a position he held at the fall of Sevastopol in September 1855. Afterwards he commanded the 2nd Division of the army in the Crimea. Barnard allowed Fenton to stay in his tent when he was up at the front. He also gave him one of his huts in Balaklava. In this photograph he is with Captain Barnard and his servants.

General Sir Harry David Jones was commissioned into the Royal Engineers in 1808 and was involved in the Walcheren Expedition and then in the Peninsular War, including the defence of Cadiz. He occupied a number of engineering posts before the Crimean War, being given command of the land forces in the Baltic with the rank of Brigadier-General. Following the successful attack upon Bomarsund he returned to the UK but was soon sent out to the Crimea, taking command of the engineers at the siege of Sevastopol. He was wounded in the forehead by a spent grape shot on the 18th June 1855 but remained in post until the fall of the Russian city.

Major General Sir George Buller joined the Rifle Brigade in 1820, rising through the grades to become a Colonel commanding a brigade in the 1st Kaffir War. He was given command of the 2nd Brigade of the Light Division in the Crimea, being wounded at the Battle of Inkerman. This incident was witnessed by Henry Clifford: 'Shortly after the cannon opened up on us, General Buller's horse was struck with round shot in the chest. I rode off to Camp and got another horse which he mounted under a tremendous fire of shell, cannon and grape; he was hardly in the saddle when I saw a cannon ball strike some yards in front of him. I called out, but he could not see it and fortunately did not move, for the cannon ball struck his horse in the chest, a little higher up than the first, and remained in the poor animal's side, giving the General a severe contusion upon the knee.' Buller was invalided home in March 1855.

Brigadier Robert Garrett was commissioned into the 2nd Regiment in 1811 and served in the Peninsular War. In 1846 he became Colonel of the 46th Regiment. Garrett arrived at Balaklava with the 46th on Wednesday 8 November. This arrival was observed by Fanny Duberly: 'They are a particularly fine looking regiment; two companies are already here. They landed, 750 strong.' Garrett was later given command of the 1st Brigade of the 4th Division.

Lieutenant Colonel Clarke Kennedy, Aide-de-Camp to the Duke of Cambridge. Aged thirty-four, the Duke of Cambridge was the grandson of George III. He had sixteen years service in the Army, mostly in staff positions. He commanded the 1st Division. During the Battle of Alma, Cambridge at first refused to advance with his division as he believed that the orders he received made no sense. A month later, at the start of the Battle of Balaklava, Raglan's ADC interpreted Lord Raglan's orders in simpler terms: 'There's a row going on down in the Balaklava Plain, and you fellows are wanted.' This time the Duke understood! He proved not to be so stupid, however, when, during the winter of 1854/5, with the troops suffering on the heights above Sevastopol he urged Raglan to withdraw the men to Balaklava where they could be more easily supplied and where they would be sheltered from the cold. When Raglan refused to do this, Cambridge resigned and returned to the UK.

Brevet Lieutenant Colonel Edmund Gilling Hallewell, Assistant Quartermaster-General, Unattached, Staff. When Fenton took Hallewell's photo, Sir John Campbell told him that if he was ever to be at the head of an army, Hallewell would be his Quartermaster-General. 'I hear his praise in everyone's mouth,' wrote Fenton. Hallewell got the chance to prove himself in that role when he joined the Kertch expedition as Deputy Adjutant-General (see Chapter 7).

A group photograph of a number of Raglan's Head Quarters staff including the French liaison officer Colonel Vico and Major the Honourable Leicester Curzon. The latter, who confusingly became Lieutenant General Sir Leicester Smyth, was Raglan's aide-de-camp and later performed the same role with General Codrington after Raglan had died. Also shown here is Lord Burghersh; an orderly; Count Revel; the interpreter, Mr Calvert; Colonel Poulett George Henry Somerset, another aide to Raglan who was his uncle; Colonel A. Hardinge; D. Prendergast; Commander Maxse and Colonel Kingscote. Sir Robert Nigel Fitzhardinge Kingscote of the Scots Fusilier Guards, was another of Raglan's relatives who served with him as an aide-de-camp, in this case he was Raglan's great-nephew.

Two photographs of *Maréchal* Aimable Jean Jacques Pélissier. An experienced officer, Pélissier took part in the invasion of Spain in 1823 to restore the Bourbon monarchy and in France's expedition to Algeria in 1830. He rose to the rank of *général de division*, and was chief-of-staff for the province of Oran. Pélissier was still in Algeria when the French forces were shipped to the Crimea but after the death of St Arnaud he was sent out to the Crimea to take over command of the army from *Maréchal* Canrobert on 16 May 1855. His successful storming of Sevastopol's Malakoff Tower on 8 September clinched victory for the Allies and resulted in him being created *duc de Malakoff* by Napoleon III. When Fenton dined with Pélissier on 6 June 1855, he found him, 'a very good personification of the French army, for he is rough in his manners, though not without a certain *bonhomie*. He cares nothing for the sacrifice of life, and does not seem troubled with scruples of any kind. His face has the expression of brutal boldness something like that of a wild boar.'

'General Bosquet giving orders to his staff.' As a young artillery officer Pierre François Joseph Bosquet served in Algeria for nineteen years from 1834 to 1853, rising through the ranks, to become a *général de division*. For the Crimean expedition Bosquet, aged forty-four, was given command of the French 2nd Division. When the respective forces settled down to the Siege of Sevastopol Bosquet was given command of two divisions which were detached as a Corps of Observation to help guard the heights on the exposed British right flank. Fenton, who spent some time with Bosquet, regarded him as 'a fine looking man with a broad face full of good temper'.

This is a photograph of General Cissé who was Bosquet's chief-of-staff. He is shown here with one of his aides.

His Royal Highness, Prince Napoleon Joseph Charles Bonaparte was the nephew of Napoleon I and was the heir to the throne of his cousin, Napoleon III. He commanded the French 3rd Division but abandoned the expedition after the Battle of Inkerman, being accused of cowardice. When he returned to Paris in January 1855, he canvassed against the war and made it known that he thought Sevastopol was 'impregnable'.

The commander of the Ottoman Army, Omar Pasha, was actually born in Croatia, then part of the Austrian empire, as Mihajlo Latas. His military career began in the Austrian Army in his father's regiment but when his father was convicted of misappropriating regimental funds Mihajlo left the Austrian Army. He converted to Islam as Omar Pasha and joined the Ottoman Army. He became the Governor of Lebanon and at the time of the Crimean War was in command of the Turkish forces in Moldavia and Wallachia, achieving two remarkable victories against the Russians. When the Allies landed in the Crimea, Omar Pasha's 35,000-man Turkish corps was concentrated in Eupatoria to guard the flank of the Allied operations against Sevastopol. He is shown here with Colonel Simmons the Queen's Commissioner attached to Omar's headquarters. He kept a private harem and employed an orchestra of Germans which accompanied him on campaign.

Ismail Pasha, originally a Hungarian called György Kmety, became a general in the Ottoman Army. Under Omar Pasha he defeated the Russian attempt to relieve Sevastopol at the Battle of Kars on 29 September 1855.

Chapter Two

Battle of the River Alma

On 5 September 1854, the combined Anglo-French fleet set sail from Scutari amid much speculation about its destination, though many had already realised that the most likely objective would be Sevastopol, the main base of the Russian Black Seas Fleet. Exactly where the 30,000 French, 27,000 British and 7,000 Turks would be landed was also a subject of much discussion. It was known that Sevastopol was defended and that a portion of the Black Seas Fleet lay there at anchor. A direct attack and amphibious assault was certain to be a costly affair and was discounted. After some discussion aboard ship St Arnaud agreed to Raglan's proposal to land thirty miles to the north of Sevastopol at Kalamita Bay where it was likely to be unopposed.

After more than a week at sea, on 14 September, the landing at Kalamita Bay began, unopposed as expected, but not unobserved. A party of Cossacks watched the Allies disembark. The Russians now knew the direction of the Allied attack and they would be waiting. In atrocious weather conditions it took two days for the troops to disembark and even longer for the rest of the equipment to be unloaded.

St Arnaud hoped to be able to begin the advance southwards towards Sevastopol on the 17th but the British burdened with 'an immense quantity of impedimenta' declared that they would not be able to move until the 19th.[1]

Between Kalamita Bay and Sevastopol were three rivers. The first of these natural barriers, the River Bulganek was crossed with little difficulty. The Russians, under Prince Menshikov, could be seen massing on the far bank of the river but, apart from a brief artillery duel, the crossing was not contested. It was at the next river, the Alma, where the Russians were waiting in strongly fortified positions overlooking the Causeway that led south to Sevastopol.

The French had reconnoitred the Alma and found it fordable right down to its mouth. They had also seen that the eastern heights were only lightly held. St Arnaud proposed that his force should tackle the heights covered by the guns of the fleet which could sail within cannon shot. With the Russians suitably distracted by the unexpected movement, the British would attack the main Russian positions on Kourgané Hill and try to turn the Russian right flank. The attack would start on the morning of 20 September.

At 05:00 hours the French advance began in silence. The British were due to begin their move two hours later but because they had had to face east during the night ready to counter a dawn attack by the Russians, Raglan had to re-position his entire force and the British were unable to advance southwards until 11:30 hours, the French having been ordered, meanwhile, to halt.

The guns of the warships opened fire shortly after midday and the advance began. The French moved in columns on a series of narrow fronts, whereas the British deployed into line across a broad front to await news that the French had surmounted the heights.

The British right front in the attack upon the Alma position was formed by Sir George Brown's Light Division slightly behind and to the right of which was De Lacy Evan's 2nd Division. Behind the Light Division was the Duke of Cambridge with the 1st Division and, even further behind and to the west, were Sir Richard English and the 3rd Division. Cathcart's 4th Division was in reserve to the east. The cavalry, in the shape of the Light Brigade guarded the extreme eastern flank.

With a general attack seemingly imminent, the Russians had set fire to the village of Burlik (or Bourliouk) to impede the Allies, should they attempt to use the Causeway as an avenue of advance. The bridge that carried the road over the Alma had also been partially destroyed.

The French succeeded in crossing the river and climbing the heights by the coast. As expected Menshikov, surprised and shocked that his left flank was being turned, despatched eight battalions accompanied by Hussars from his reserves to meet this threat.

As the French attack developed, Raglan at last ordered his men to move. Those orders were to advance directly against the Russian positions. The men, who had been waiting for an hour-and-a-half under artillery fire, scrambled to their feet and formed into a two-deep line almost two miles long. The men of the 2nd and Light divisions waded through the river and into the face of the Russian artillery, the riflemen of the Rifle Brigade skirmishing in front.

Subjected to heavy and well-directed fire the leading British divisions started to lose cohesion, and the ordered ranks began to fall into disarray. To make matters worse Sir George Brown had not allowed enough space for his division to fully deploy so when the 2nd Division tried to move up alongside the Light Division there was not enough room for every regiment to pass to the left of the burning village of Burlik. Evans had to split his command, sending General Adams with the 41st and 49th Regiments and Turner's battery of artillery round the right-hand side of the village.

Now the troops had to cross the river, as Sergeant Timothy Gowing of the 7th Regiment in Codrington's Fusilier Brigade of the Light Division recalled: 'Our men were falling fast; into the river we dashed, nearly up to our armpits, with ammunition and rifles on the top of our heads to keep them dry, scrambled out the best way we could, and commenced to ascend the hill. From east to west the enemy's batteries were served with rapidity, hence we were enveloped in smoke on what may be called the glacis. We were only about 600 yards from the mouths of the guns, the thunderbolts of war were, therefore, not far apart, and death loves a crowd.'[2]

The various brigades of the 2nd and Light divisions had now become inextricably mixed with the 95th Regiment of Pennefather's brigade having joined the Light Division and the 19th Regiment of Buller's brigade having gone forward with Codrington's brigade.

In front of the British, on the lower slopes of the hill, Russian skirmishers found easy targets amongst the crowded and confused ranks. But as the red coats climbed onto the southern bank of the Alma, the skirmishers pulled back. This allowed the Russian gunners to fire without the danger of hitting their own men, and the round shot and common shell of the early stages of the battle was now exchanged for canister.

All order had been lost in crossing the river but the fire from the Russian guns was so intense that to stop and dress ranks before making the push up the hill would have been suicidal. So the commanding officer of the 7th Regiment, Colonel Lacy Yea shouted to his men, 'Never mind forming, for God's sake … come on, come on, men! Come on anyhow!'[3]

The ragged British line was next to be assailed by two strong columns of Russian infantry. The column on the British left was met by the Rifle Brigade and the 19th and 23rd Regiments and that on the right, the west, was halted by the 7th Regiment. Despite his earlier command, Colonel Yea ordered his men into line to face the Russian column. Though considerably outnumbered by the two battalions of the Kazansky Regiment, the 7th stood their ground and the Russian counter-attack faltered.

The rest of the two leading British divisions continued on up towards the principle Russian defensive work, the Great Redoubt. The Russian gunners in the redoubt held their fire until the attackers were within 300 yards. Then they opened fire, tearing more holes in the already loose lines of infantry. Ironically, it was because the British troops no longer presented a solid front that the fire of the Russian guns was not as effective as might have been expected at such close quarters.

Finally the redcoats reached the Great Redoubt. 'General Codrington waved his hat then rode straight at one of the embrasures, and leapt his grey Arab into the breast work; others breathless, were soon beside him,' continued Sergeant Gowing. 'Up we went, step by step, but with a horrible carnage … a cheer and a charge brought us to the top of the hill.'[4]

As they rushed over the parapets of the Great Redoubt, the men of the Light Division expected to be assailed by the defenders but to their amazement all they saw was the Russian artillery teams retreating with their guns. The Great Redoubt, the main Russian strongpoint was in British hands, but the Battle of the Alma was far from over.

Though the Russians had withdrawn from the summit of Kourgané Hill, there was still fighting continuing elsewhere on the battlefield. The 7th Regiment was still locked in a terrible fire-fight with the Kazansky Regiment and the French were heavily engaged on the plateau to the west. A counter-attack by the Russians to recapture the redoubt was likely and the British needed to quickly consolidate. But the 1st Division, which should have been close in support of the first line, was still crossing the river.

Alone and unsupported on the hill, the Light Division was soon to see the 3,000-strong Vladimir Regiment bearing down on them. Exactly what followed next has never been fully explained. It seems that someone called out not to fire on the advancing column as it was French. Though a ragged fire was opened up by some on the unidentified column a bugler of the 19th Regiment sounded the ceasefire. This was followed, inexplicably, by another bugle call – 'Retire'. Who ordered these instructions, or why, is unknown but the troops obeyed and the Great Redoubt, captured at such a great cost was meekly abandoned. Only part of the 23rd Regiment remained on the hill.[5]

Now, though, the 1st Division had at last begun to mount the hill. The first part of the battle had definitely been won by the Russians. They were back in possession of Kourgané Hill and the British infantry had once again to climb up the hill. The situation this time though was a little different. The Russians had withdrawn most of their guns from the Great Redoubt during the first attack and now two 9-pounders of Major Turner's battery were in position on a knoll within range of the heights.

The advance of the 1st Division – the Guards Brigade to the right and the Highland Brigade on the left – was truly memorable with the bobbing tall bearskins and swirling multi-coloured kilts.

The Grenadier Guards, the Scots Fusilier Guards and the Coldstream Guards aimed directly for the Great Redoubt. As they approached the summit of the hill the Russians unleashed hundreds of soldiers, who swarmed over the parapets of the retaken redoubt and poured a shattering volley of musket fire downwards. The party of the 23rd Regiment was smashed and rushed down the hill, crashing into the advancing Scots Guards with such force that the line was broken in many places. The Scots Guards faltered, and when they were forty yards from the redoubt the Russians mounted a massive bayonet charge. The Scots Guards were forced to retreat and they did so stopping only when they reached the Alma. Almost 200 of them lay dead on the slope

A large gap now existed between the Grenadiers and the Coldstream Guards and though the Russians tried to exploit this gap, the remnants of the 23rd, with the re-formed 33rd and 19th and 95th regiments, returned to the attack. At this time Sir Colin Campbell arrived with the Highland Brigade.

The determination of the Guards combined with the rapid and steady volleys of the Highlanders with their Minié rifles was added to by men of Lacy Yea's brigade who had at last turned back two of the four battalions of the Kazansky Regiment, thanks to the intervention of the 55th Regiment which had been brought forward by Evans.

Though the two other Kazansky battalions rallied, being supported by the Vladimir Regiment, the tide had turned against the Russians. The Highlanders came up on the left of the Guards.

'We at once opened fire,' wrote one Highlander, the men firing by files as they advanced. On getting nearer, the front company of the Russian Regiment opposite to us, a very large one, brought down their bayonets, and I thought were about to charge us; but on our giving a cheer, they at once faced about and retired.'[6] The British infantry seized the Great Redoubt and, with the Royal Artillery firing at their backs, the Russians retreated leaving the Allies in command of the hilltop.

Now was the chance to turn the Russian withdrawal into a rout. The British cavalry moved forward and had begun to take prisoners but Raglan ordered them to halt. There would be no pursuit. Raglan's reasons for not following up the victory have been much condemned as the Russians had placed great faith in their ability to hold the Alma position and were not only demoralised by their defeat but also disorganised. 'He then sat there rejoicing at his victory over what he imagined to be the advanced guard of our army,' wrote one Russian survivor of the battle, 'his mistake saved us and Sevastopol. It is frightful to think what might have happened had it not been for this cardinal error of the enemy's.'[7]

Yet Raglan was in enemy territory with little idea what lay ahead of him. A pursuit might well have won the campaign for him but equally a pursuit, by its very nature, is difficult to control. If his cavalry had charged off unsupported towards Sevastopol it might have found itself in considerable difficulty if the Russians had rallied. Raglan played his hand cautiously and it is hard to blame him for that.

The Allied army was initially sent to Besika Bay near the southern entrance to the Dardanelles. The stated objective was to help defend Constantinople from the Russians but Besika Bay was 190 miles from Constantinople. If the Russians were to attack across the Black Sea they would have reached Constantinople long before the Allied fleet. The Allies, therefore, moved up to Constantinople. These two photographs show, above, the Coldstream Guards, and below, the Grenadier Guards at Scutari on the eastern bank of the Bosphorus. In the background of the former photograph is the great Barracks of Selim III, whilst in the latter can be seen the Hagia Sophia and the Blue Mosque of Istanbul across the Bosphorus. It was in the Selim Barracks that Florence Nightingale established her hospital in November 1854. From Scutari the British and French armies moved to Varna on the Black Sea from where they could strike against the Russians. These two photographs were taken by James Robertson in the spring of 1854. The smart white trousers of the Guards are in stark contrast to the ragged clothing the troops would be pictured in during the harsh Crimean winter that was to come.

'We are now in a camp at Scutari,' wrote Lieutenant Colonel Frederick Stephenson of the Scots Guards in May 1854. 'Our position is quite lovely, and although there is an enormous barrack [the Selim Barracks] close by capable of holding 7,000 men, I am very glad it did not fall our lot to be quartered there. It is a fine imposing building, but the filth and the stench of the rooms is quite beyond description and it swarms with fleas.'

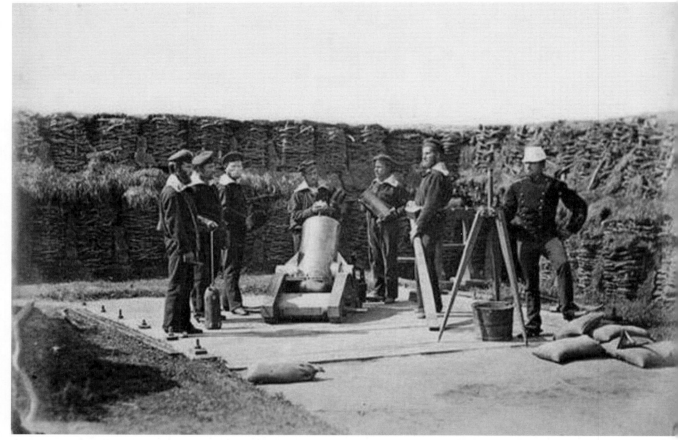

One of Carol Szathmari's photographs from the early stages of the war. This is a shot of a mortar battery at Calafat on the Danube. When war broke out between Russia and Turkey Russian forces advanced down the Danube valley. On 28 January 1854 they reached Calafat, which was held by a strong body of troops under Ahmed Pasha. The city was besieged by the Russians under the command of General Iosif Romanovich Anrep. The siege lasted until May. With his force crippled with disease, Anrep was forced to withdraw.

(*Facing page*) Shown here are Major General Sir R. Dacres, Captain Hamley and Colonel Adye. Captain (later Lieutenant Colonel) Edward Hamley wrote about his experiences in the Crimea and described the conditions the troops encountered in Kalamita Bay: 'At night, the rain came down in torrents, and the troops on the beach were drenched … The surf was dashing very heavily on the sand, though it was too dark to see. Fires made of broken boats and rafts were lit along the beach, and a voice hailed us authoritatively to put back and not attempt to land, or we should go to pieces.'

As a Lieutenant Colonel, Richard Dacres was in command of the Royal Horse Artillery attached to the Cavalry Division when the troops sailed for the Crimea. At Alma Dacres brought his guns into action at the moment when the fight for the possession of the Great Redoubt hung in the balance and, according to De Lacy Evans, 'opened their fire immediately to the right and left, against the retiring and confused masses of the Enemy, which produced a very destructive effect'. Later, at the Battle of Balaklava, the commander of the Royal Artillery, Brigadier-General Fox-Strangways, was killed and Dacres took over command of all the artillery in the Crimea, retaining that post until the end of the war. Dacres was promoted to Colonel in February 1855, Brigadier-General the following month and Major General on 29 June.

Captain Fay on General Bosquet's staff. The French duly set off on the 19th, as Captain Fay recounted: 'At around six o'clock, having eaten soup, the right wing got under way, whilst the remainder of the French Army, under arms, prepared to leave their bivouacs, when the marshal [St Arnaud] was informed that the English had not left at the hour agreed the day before, and were not yet able to do it. He immediately sent an order to General Bosquet to suspend his march … The General, stopped in his tracks, expressed his displeasure at the slowness of our allies'.

Shown here is Major Percy Arthur Butler of the 28th Regiment which was in Sir W. Eyre's left brigade of Sir Richard England's Division which formed the second line alongside the Duke of Cambridge's 1st Division at the Alma. Butler survived the Crimea and on 2 March 1858 he was made a Lieutenant Colonel by brevet. Most of Fenton's Crimean photographs were portraits, and most of those were of officers. The reasons for this were that it he would be able to sell such photographs more easily to wealthy officers than poor rankers, plus he needed the help of officers to get his photographic van around the difficult Crimean terrain.

Also of the 28th Regiment was Captain Mottram Andrews, pictured here outside his tent. Andrews entered the Army as Ensign in the 28th Regiment in 1825. He was promoted to Lieutenant in 1828 and Captain in 1843. He was present during the siege of Sebastopol in 1855 but, as of 9 October 1855, *The London Gazette* informs us that Major Mottram Andrews had been retired on full-pay, 'to be Lieutenant-Colonel in the Army, the rank being honorary only'.

Two officers of the 47th Regiment. The 47th, along with the 30th, 55th, 95th, formed part of De Lacy's 2nd Division. They passed by the burning village of Burlik, crossed the river and the bridge: 'But this was not easily done,' observed one officer, 'for we were completely under the Enemy. Every man & movement exposed to their view, & to a continuous shower of every species of Cannon, Shot or Missile, directed with too accurate aim, such perhaps as few of the most experienced soldiers have witnessed.'

Lieutenant-Colonel Charles John Woodford, of the Rifle Brigade. Woodford was mentioned by Lord Raglan in his despatch back to the UK on the Battle of the Alma. Woodford was later killed leading a charge at the Siege of Cawnpore during the Indian Mutiny of 1857. One of the six lancet windows in the north transept in Westminster Abbey was filled with stained glass in his memory. The men of the Rifle Brigade were distinguished by their green jackets and trousers that contrasted so sharply with the rest of the red-coated British infantry. Unlike the white belts and shiny buttons of the Line infantry, those of the Rifles were black, as were the knapsacks and ammunition pouches.

Captain Francis Baring, 1st Battalion Fusilier Guards, was Deputy Assistant Quartermaster General, attached to the Light Division. Though he survived the Battle of Alma unscathed he was severely wounded at the Battle of Inkerman on 5 November 1854. He recovered from this to take part in the siege of Sevastopol but was again wounded on 19 August 1855.

The arrival of the artillery proved to be one of the turning points in the battle. Shown here are Captain Thomas Longworth Dames (left) and below Lieutenant Shadwell Grylls (or Grills) of the Royal Horse Artillery much as they would have appeared at the Battle of the Alma, though by the time this photograph had been taken there had been a slight change in the RHA uniform, in that his blue cloth shell jacket had a single row of buttons where previously it had three. The jacket was decorated with gold or yellow cord frogging. The busby was made of bearskin (other ranks having sealskin). This had a scarlet bag and gold or yellow worsted cap lines. Other ranks carried a round, blue painted, wooden water bottle on a bridle leather strap over the right shoulder together with a canvas haversack. Over the left shoulder was a whitened buff leather shoulder belt with a black leather pouch. A light cavalry pattern sword was suspended from a whitened buff leather waist belt with a brass snake clasp.

Captain Lord Balgonie of the Grenadier Guards. Though the Battle of the Alma is notable for the disorder of the attacking troops, the exception was the Grenadier Guards. Their advance was described by Alexander Kinglake: 'The Grenadiers were a body of men so well instructed, and so skilfully handled, that in working their way through the enclosures they were able to preserve all the essential elements of their line-formation.' Born in 1831, Alexander Leslie-Melville, Viscount Balgonie died in 1857 still suffering from the effects of serving in the Crimea. He described how tough the situation was during the winter of 1854 even for an officer of the Guards: 'Having been 2 nights out of bed, he flatters himself that he is in for a good snooze and turns in at 8 o'clock. At 9 he is waked up with the pleasing intelligence that "an officer has been hit in the trenches, and that he must fill his place," or that, "the enemy is threatening our rear".'

'The Russians had formed a line in advance of their breast-work, and were thus able to resist our attack with vigour,' wrote a Guards officer, 'but after a volley from the front rank, our Grenadiers began their slow and steady advance, the rear rank firing while the front rank loaded.' This photograph is of twenty-five-years-old Captain Henry William Verschoyle of the Grenadier Guards taken some time after the Battle of Alma. He was later wounded, on 5 September 1855, at the siege of Sevastopol. He remained in the Grenadier Guards for the rest of his Army service, reaching the rank of Lieutenant Colonel. He died in 1870.

This photograph shows Captain Cunninghame of the 42nd Highland Regiment much as he would have looked at this early stage of the campaign in almost full dress (less his bonnet). Cunninghame was invalided home before the end of the war. He died of fever contracted in the trenches in front of Sevastopol at Malta on his way back to the UK on 5 September 1855.

French Zouaves seated in the centre with infantry of the line standing either side. The French attack upon the Russian left was a success due, so one Russian officer wrote, to the infantry's Minié rifles, 'I say "the deadly rifled guns," because each bullet hit its mark.' It is claimed that all the mounted Russian officers were wounded by the French rifles. The other key factor was the cannonade from the French ships. The Minsk Regiment, which was placed on the extreme left of the Russian line was virtually destroyed by the French naval bombardment.

'Lieutenant-Colonel Lord Burghersh, CB.' Lord Burghersh, or more correctly Francis Fane 12th Earl of Westmorland, still a Major at the time of the Battle of Alma, was the man that was given the responsibility for taking Lord Raglan's victory despatch back to London. In that despatch Burghersh was praised for his 'zeal, intelligence, and gallantry'. As a result when he returned to the Crimea it was as a Lieutenant Colonel and aide to the Duke of Cambridge.

Chapter Three

Balaklava

The British were as stunned by their victory at the Alma as the Russians and instead of the vigorous pursuit which could have destroyed the Russian army, the victors remained on the ground they had so dearly won. The road to Sevastopol, though, was now open. Its defences were far from strong enough to repel a full-scale assault and the defending troops had just been beaten with the loss of 5,709 men.

Whilst the dead were being buried Raglan and St Arnaud discussed the operation to move upon Sevastopol. The original plan had been to attack Sevastopol from the north side, or Severnya, but it was learnt that a major outwork holding forty-seven guns, the Star Fort, protected the landward approaches on the northern side. Further defences had been hurriedly thrown up around the Severnya. Menshikov had also ordered ships of the Black Sea Fleet to be scuttled across the harbour entrance which meant that the Allied warships would not be able to enter the harbour to lend their support to any landward attack. The Russians had also built redoubts to defend the passage of the third river to be crossed on the approach to Sevastopol, the River Belbek.

These difficulties could be overcome but what was probably the factor which induced Raglan and St Arnaud to change their plans was that they could not transport their siege equipment and supplies necessary to sustain their armies all the way from Kalamita Bay. They needed somewhere much closer and the open beaches along the coast north of Sevastopol would be dangerously exposed to attack by the Russians. So the decision was made to march round Sevastopol to the south to a narrow, and more easily defendable, inlet of Balaklava harbour which was some eight miles from Sevastopol.

The British were the first to arrive at Balaklava on 26 September, led by an unescorted Lord Raglan. The bay was said to be undefended but an old Genoese fort on the heights to the east of the harbour was held by a small garrison and Raglan was fired upon by the fort's mortars. The Rifle Brigade was sent up the heights to clear the fort.

The French arrived the next day, with St Arnaud, who had been feeling increasingly unwell, having handed over command to General Canrobert. Two days later Marshal St Arnaud died, the consequence of cancer of the bowel.[8]

It was immediately evident that the small harbour could not accommodate the ships of both nations. The French, therefore, moved westwards along the coast to two adjacent harbours at Kazach Bay and Kamiesh Bay on the Kamiesh peninsula. Together these two harbours provided the French with a far more spacious base than Balaklava.

As well as being cramped and confined, Balaklava was situated on the right flank of the new Allied positions. The Russians could not attack the French at Kamiesh as that would expose their rear to the British, but Balaklava could be assaulted from the north without such concerns.

Nevertheless, it was the Allies who were on the offensive and the garrison of Sevastopol expected to be attacked at any moment. Raglan was for an immediate assault upon the city, but his chief engineer, General Sir John Burgoyne advised against an assault until the city's defences had been reduced. Views were certainly split on the subject. Lord Cathcart, whose 4th Division occupied the heights above the eastern approaches to the city wrote to Raglan: '... the place is only enclosed by a thing like a low park wall, not in good repair ... I am sure I could walk into it, with scarcely the loss of a man, at night or an hour before daybreak ... we could leave our packs and run into it even in open day, only risking a few shots while we passed the redoubt'.[9]

Raglan chose to ignore Burgoyne's advice and he went to the French with his proposal for an assault upon Sevastopol before its defences, which the Russians were working hard to improve, became too formidable. Canrobert would have none of it. He believed that Sevastopol was already too secure and that the only way the city could be taken was by a formal siege.

The Allies, therefore, had to wait for the siege guns to be unloaded. Meanwhile, Raglan had to make sure that Balaklava was well guarded against a move by Menshikov who had decided not to place his field army in Sevastopol but instead to allow it the freedom to manoeuvre against the Allies. The little harbour became incredibly busy as the British encampment became established.

Balaklava is a deep-water anchorage flanked by hills on either side with another small hill by the village of Kadikoi which overlooked the approaches from the north. Kadikoi was in a valley, which became known as the South Valley to the north of which were the Causeway Heights. Beyond these was another valley, the North Valley and then the Fedioukine Heights. To the north-west the Sapouné Heights, flanked by the ruins of the Old City of Inkerman, led to the Sevastopol plateau.

Sevastopol itself was garrisoned by 16,000 men at the time of the arrival of the Allies and the defences on its landward side amounted to 172 guns. By the time the Allies were ready to begin siege operations, the garrison had been increased by the addition of twelve of Menshikov's battalions to a strength of 38,000, and mounted on Sevastopol's landward fortifications were 341 pieces of artillery.[10]

The Allies were allowed to establish their siege lines undisturbed by the enemy, forming a semi-circle around Sevastopol's southern perimeter. Raglan's force was deployed with the 3rd and 4th divisions touching the main French body to the west. To the north east was the 2nd Division which occupied the ground as far as what became known as Shell Hill. Southwards from here was the 1st Division, the right of which rested on Sapouné ridge where two further French divisions formed what was called the 'Army of Observation', whose task was to guard the Allied rear by 'observing' the Balaklava plain. It was from these positions that the Allies prepared to bombard Sevastopol.

A naval bombardment had been planned to commence at the same time but a last minute change of plan meant that Vice Admiral James Dundas had to completely re-organise his ships and they were unable to bring their guns into action against the Sevastopol forts until the early afternoon.

The British breaching batteries brought their fire to bear on what was termed the Flagstaff Bastion and the powerful Redan bastion, eventually demolishing and then blowing up the Redan, possibly because a large magazine had been struck. This tore a large gap in the city's defences but no advantage was taken of it.

The Russians responded vigorously, hitting a French magazine which ignited with a massive explosion. This discouraged the French gunners and their guns remained silent for the rest of the day. Fire from the Russian Telegraph Battery on the cliffs to the north of Sevastopol also proved effective, driving the British warships from their anchored positions.

The bombardment continued over the following days, with little noticeable diminution in the determination of the defenders to resist.

Already the ill-prepared and ill-equipped British army was suffering from the ravages of disease and winter was fast approaching. Winters in the Crimea could be very wet and cold and tents provided the troops only shelter. By 23 October Raglan's force had shrunk to little more than 18,000 effectives. Sevastopol had to be taken, and taken soon.

A view of Balaklava, showing the old Genoese fort at the entrance to the harbour. 'We went skirmishing up the hills and more troops were sent to crown the heights on both sides,' wrote Lieutenant-Colonel Arthur Lawrence of the 2nd Battalion of the Rifles. 'From the heights in front I witnessed this mimic fight for the fort was so small it hardly deserved the name. Our artillery battered it on one side and the "Agamemnon" fired into it from the sea, while the Rifles fired into it from the heights on both sides.' The officer in charge of the fort, having done his duty, then surrendered.

(*Facing page, below*) Robertson's photograph of the French base at Kamiesch Bay. It was far more suitable for landing supplies than Balaklava. Large warehouses, slaughterhouses, private shops and trading stalls were soon established around the broad horseshoe bay. The various shops were arranged in streets which were given names. There were bars and brothels, hotels and restaurants. This included one where the soldiers could pay a fixed price for a three-day orgy of food, wine and women, all brought in from France. The French also had much better provision for the wounded or sick soldiers. 'The wounded are carefully laid on beds in rows, then come the sick and so on,' observed Captain Portal of the British 4th Light Dragoons, 'everything is clean and nice; the man's name and complaint on a piece of paper over his bed, as if he were in a barrack hospital.' (*Courtesy of the King's Own Royal Regiment Museum*)

George Shaw Lefevre's photograph of HMS *Leander* at the entrance to Balaklava harbour. *Leander* was a fifty-gun fourth rate launched in 1848 and was involved in the early operations in the Crimea. When the Allied landing began at Kalamita a Royal Navy force was despatched to seize the nearby port of Eupatoria. The port surrendered without offering any resistance and a small force of Royal Marines occupied the place and fortified it. The Russians counter-attacked on 19 September and 12 October 1854. As a result *Leander* was sent to help the 400 marines, landing 100 of her crew. Eventually Eupatoria was garrisoned by more than 25,000 men, mostly Turks. *Leander* later became the centre of much attention in Balaklava when Captain William Peel's quarters were taken over by Lord George Paget's beautiful new bride, Agnes. Amongst those that went to see her were Lord Raglan and the head of the Turkish Army, Omar Pasha. *Leander* was converted to screw propulsion in 1861 and was sold in 1867.

The following are some of Fenton's photographs of Balaklava. The first of these shows 'Cossack Bay'. At its widest point the harbour was less than 300 yards across and from the harbour entrance to the head of the harbour was about three-quarters of a mile. 'The stench along the waterside is very bad,' wrote Fenton shortly after his arrival at Balaklava. 'All the dead oxen and horses floating about the harbour have been towed out to sea. Do what they will, there is an immense quantity of putrefying matter which cannot be got rid of. The ground is everywhere thickly strewn with barley, the harbour is crammed with ships lying closer than in any docks, many of them empty, doing nothing themselves and keeping others from discharging their cargo.'

(*Facing page*) This is a general view of the town of Balaklava. Soon after their arrival all the buildings in Balaklava were taken over by the British and many of the inhabitants, who were Greeks, were forced to leave. Captain Jean-Jules Herbé, wrote to his family about Balaklava: 'The shacks constructed in the little port are full of goods for sale but everything is piled up pell-mell, without any order or attraction for the buyer. I am astonished that the English chose it as their supply base in preference to Kamiesh.'

With as many as 150 ships in Balaklava, it was said that there were more ships in such a confined space than anywhere else in the world at that time. 'The harbour is crammed with ships as tight as they can be packed,' wrote Temple Godman of the 5th Dragoon Guards, 'and the stench of harbour and town is horrible ... I cannot think why they crowd this place so with ships, should a fire occur they can't possibly escape, and some are full of shell and powder and the sailors often drunk.' This photograph of Fenton's is looking towards the sea with the harbour Commandant's house in the foreground.

The British troops formed their encampments around Balaklava. A mile and a half north of Balaklava was the village of Kadikoi and on the hill nearby was the Guards camp. This is a photo of the Guards camp on a hill which, inevitably, was labelled 'Guards' Hill'. The tents were described by one soldier as 'very comfortable in dry weather, but most uncomfortable in wet weather, where so many are crowded into one tent. First your head must not touch it. Then your comrades coming in wet, tired and covered in mud – you get a good share of wet and mud from them if you are not in the same state yourself, so that it is continually uncomfortable. If you sit down it must be in a doubled up position with your head nearly touching your knees. If you lie down you get kicked and trod on by all comers.'

An essential service that was established at Balaklava was the postal service. It was set up in this house, the ground floor of which was a stable. This photograph was the first one taken by Fenton in the Crimea, on 15 March 1855.

The postal service was under the direction of Mr Angel, the Post Master General. Angel promised Fenton a hut to stay in but relations between the two were not good. When Fenton asked 'Well, Angel, when do you expect the next mail?', Angel replied, 'Damn the mail!'

A hospital was also established at Balaklava. It is shown here in this general view of Balaklava. There were soon far too many casualties and sick to be accommodated in the hospital and ships were used to transport the men to the hospital at Scutari. 'The sick and wounded were placed indiscriminately on the decks, to the great risk of the wounded,' recalled a naval surgeon, James Peters, on board HMS *Vulcan*, 'for with diseases such as cholera and dysentery extensively prevailing, the atmosphere becomes quickly tainted … great distress was experienced from want of urinals and bed pans, one only of each being on board.'

(*Facing page*) Above is a view of the Cattle Pier and below is a photograph of the Ordnance Wharf at Balaklava where the heavy guns were unloaded. 'The camp is a wonderful sight,' observed Mrs Fanny Duberly, the wife of Henry Duberly the paymaster of the 8th Hussars who arrived at Balaklava on 4 October. 'The sailors are all landed & employed a hundred at a time hauling up the heavy guns. The largest requires 18 or 20 horses.' Balaklava harbour was also described by Lady Alicia Blackwood: 'As to Balaklava harbour, it is most extraordinary, a wonder of the world; its narrow entrance, its high rocky sides, deep waters, and beautiful anchorage for ships. I have never seen anything which has struck me so powerfully for a moment of British power, energy and wealth, as the appearance of things in Balaklava and the camp. It seems as if a part of England has been transported bodily to the Crimea. No picture conveys an idea of it. The railway running along to the harbour with its locomotives, and a capital military road running for miles in several directions is now covered with strings of mules and wagons. Warehouses, shops, cafes – English, French, and Greek – are crowded with customers, and the whole place is alive like a series of populous towns in the industrial towns of England, swarming with people full of energy and work, beyond the ordinary energy of peace at home.'

Whilst the Russians were hurriedly improving the defences of Sevastopol, Balaklava harbour was a hive of activity as increasing numbers of guns and ammunition was shipped out to help the besieging forces. This is another of Fenton's photographs of the Ordnance Wharf, showing cannon balls and gun barrels.

Roger Fenton's photographic van which he used as a travelling darkroom, shown here with his assistant Marcus Sparling. Fenton experienced considerable difficulty moving his van around the hilly terrain between Balaklava and the Allied camp on the Sevastopol plateau. Until the van could be taken up to the front Fenton transported his equipment round on horseback and used officers' tents to develop his photographs, with limited success.

Sevastopol's main fortifications were built to defend the harbour from an attack from the sea and to defend the place from the land there were just two stone-built towers, the Malakov being the principal one. The rest of the defences were mainly just earthworks strengthened with a few outworks and bastions, the principle ones known as the Redan and the Flagstaff Bastion. The Russian works were screened by rifle-pits from which sorties were frequently made against the Allied trenches. This photograph shows the Allied camp on the plateau before Sevastopol. Raglan described the Russian positions at Sevastopol: 'The position which the enemy occupy on the south side of Sevastopol is not that of a fortress, but rather of an army in an entrenched camp on very strong ground, where an apparently unlimited number of heavy guns, amply provided with gunners and ammunition, are mounted.' This photograph shows the Allied camp on the plateau before Sevastopol.

A view of Sevastopol. Though difficult to see, Fenton's caption for this photograph states that it shows the Redan, Malakoff Tower and the Mamelon Vert. The Mamelon Vert was a small hill about 400 yards in front of the Malakoff Tower. Colonel Shadforth can be seen seated here in the foreground. The lack of features in the distance photos of Fenton's were explained by him as being because the ground was 'but wide stretches of open country.' He was critical of the sketches and paintings published in the newspapers in the UK which gave a false impression of the terrain.

The bombardment of Sevastopol began at 06:30 hours on 17 October, observed by Captain Samuel Enderby Gordon of the Royal Artillery: 'The roar of some 300 Cannon and smoke created by them was incessant for about half an hour. The smoke then began to clear off and the Round Tower (the Malakhov) opposite us struck work being battered about the Top and the guns dismounted.' The photograph here is that of a distant view of Sevastopol with the Mamelon and Malakoff Tower, the lines of Captain Gordon's Battery (of twenty-seven guns) is in the middle distance.

This is a similar view to the previous one, this one being labelled 'artillery waggons, view looking towards Balaklava. View of artillery camp with caissons, barracks, tents, and horses.' In total the British batteries mounted seventy-two guns and the French fifty-three. These numbers would increase considerably as the siege progressed, 'Thus began the greatest artillery battle the world had ever seen,' remarked one historian.

Robertson's photograph of one of the Lancaster gun batteries. Six of the British siege guns were 8-inch 'Lancaster' guns. These 68-pounders were taken from two Royal Navy warships and were manned by men of the Royal Naval Brigade. This brigade operated under its own officers and reported independently back to the Admiralty. The men of the brigade came from all the warships in the British fleet, with the five largest ships contributing 200 each and the smaller ones a proportionate number. This produced a force of over 2,400 sailors, 2,000 marines and nearly 160 guns. The men were mostly deployed in the defence of Balaklava but a detachment of Royal Marine Artillery, under Major Alexander manned the guns in the batteries, supported by two companies of marines. The Lancaster guns were the first rifled artillery guns used in warfare. Instead of the spherical shells fired by other guns, the Lancaster's ammunition was conical shaped. Each shell was eighteen inches long and contained an explosive charge of twelve pounds of gunpowder. With a range of 6,500 yards, much was expected of these weapons but their performance did not match those expectations. They were placed in two 'half-sunken batteries' on the Victoria Ridge, approximately 2,800 yards from Sevastopol. (*Courtesy of the King's Own Royal Regiment Museum*)

This is Jean-Charles Langlois' photo of the Canrobert Redoubt. 'The French open all at once, about 4 or 5 times a day, every gun they have at the same instant' wrote Major Henry Clifford, 'and keep it up for an hour or so without intermission. It is awful and splendid to see the French open on the left in this way, make the Russian batteries dance with shot and shell.' Captain Cuninghame saw the Russian response. 'All of a sudden ... every available gun and mortar in Sevastopol seem to have been discharged at the French right, all loaded with shell and some with 13 or 16 small ones ... I am sure there must have been 100 shells in the air at once; the Russians have a nasty trick of loading one big mortar with a number of small shells generally 16 in number, these spread in every direction and must be extremely inconvenient to those against whom they are directed. Fortunately for us they reserve these delicate little attentions for the French.'

In February work began on a railway from Balaklava to the Sevastopol plateau. The work was conducted by navvies sent out from Britain. The railway was completed by the end of March 1855. No longer would the ordinary soldiers have to carry provisions all the way from the harbour and this considerably improved both the condition and the morale of the soldiers. At first the wagons were drawn by horses or mules assisted by stationary steam engines at steep places. Later at least five locomotives were shipped out to the Crimea, the names of three are known – *Alliance*, *Victory* and *Swan*. By the end of April the railway was handling 240 tons of ammunition and stores per day which had previously taken some 2,000 horses.

Shown here are railway officials, Swan, Cadell, Middleton, Howse and Kellock. Though Fenton transported his photographic equipment in a covered wagon, he needed a horse to travel around the various Allied posts. He had not anticipated this and he arrived in the Crimea with no horse furniture. He was, however, lent a saddle and bridle by Mr Swan. In recompense, as it were, Fenton took his picture for posterity (or for profit).

A group of Tartar labourers shown here at work repairing the roadway at Balaklava in front of the store of the 14th Regiment. The Muslim Tartar population of the Crimea had no love for their Russian masters and they saw the Allies as liberators and the Turks as their spiritual brothers. Shortly after the Allies landed thousands of Tartars rallied to their support and many offered their services to the invading army. Many others rode around the Crimea robbing and threatening the Christian Russian landowners and destroying churches. This had a negative effect, as it engendered considerable support for the Tsar's armies.

Looking towards Mackenzie's Heights (named after a wealthy landowner of Scottish origin) with tents of the 33rd Regiment in the foreground. 'We have now been at the Town like 'Blazes' since the 17th & with very little Effect,' considered Major George Mundy of the 33rd Regiment. 'We are bombarding a place like Woolwich, cram full of Cannon, shot etc., etc., and beautifully served. I believe we shall take it in time but not with Artillery, the bayonet I fear will have to do the work.'

Florence Nightingale was probably the most famous individual of the Crimean War, even though her major contribution to the care of the sick and wounded was not actually in the Crimea at all. Florence and her team of nurses began operating at Selimiye Barracks at Scutari, Istanbul, in November 1854. Though undoubtedly Nightingale and her nurses helped comfort thousands of British soldiers, death rates actually rose during that first winter of the war, with ten times more men dying from disease than battle wounds. Part of the problem was that Nightingale did not understand that poor hygiene was the main cause of the spread of disease. It was only when a Sanitary Commission was sent out to the Crimea that death rates began to decline.

(*Left*) Conditions at Balaklava had become terrible, with the men dying through ill-managed and inadequate hospitals. Though Florence Nightingale did not fully appreciate how infections were spread she called for the establishment of a Sanitary Commission. This was adopted by the Government and a Sanitary Commission was sent out to the Crimea to investigate, arriving at Scutari in March 1855. The Commission consisted of Dr John Sutherland, Dr Hector Gavin (who died in the Crimea), and Robert Rawlinson a civil engineer. This is a photograph of Rawlinson, whom Fenton incorrectly calls Sir Henry, not Robert.

(*Right*) Shortly after the arrival of the Sanitary Commissioners at Balaklava, Dr Gavin died and was replaced by Dr Milroy. The Commissioners also took with them the Borough Engineer and three sanitary inspectors from Liverpool. Above is a photograph of Dr Sutherland. Sutherland was a member of the Board of Health.

Ismail Pasha is shown here with his Turkish infantry bodyguards. William Russell saw the Turkish troops that were posted on the Fedioukine Heights: 'Overlooking the road to Balaklava, a party of 2,000 Turks were busily engaged casting up earthworks for redoubts. These poor fellows worked most diligently and indefatigably, though they had been exposed to the greatest privations. For some mysterious reason the Turkish government sent a body of soldiers of only two years' service, the latest levies of the Porte, many belonging to the non-belligerent class of barbers, tailors, and small shopkeepers. Still they were patient, hardy, and strong.' These troops would later be accused of cowardice, somewhat unfairly, at the Battle of Balaklava, yet as Russell observed, from the Battle of the Alma up to 10 October, the rations for the whole of this force amounted to just two biscuits each.

(*Facing page*) Looking towards Balaklava, with the Turkish camp in the distance to the right. Below are a number of Turkish troops accompanying Ismail Pasha. The British were shocked at the poor conditions that the Turkish troops had to endure. One officer described them as, 'Poorly fed and dressed in rags, they were the most wretched specimens of humanity.'

Chapter Four

The Battle of Balaklava

For the first few days following the opening salvos of the bombardment of Sevastopol the siege had continued with little interference by Prince Menshikov's mobile army. There had been a few scares with the Russian's testing the alertness of the Allied outposts, and Raglan had called out all his men, but the Russians had not pressed home an attack. Yet Menshikov's force of twenty-five battalions of infantry, thirty-four squadrons of cavalry and seventy-eight guns, was creeping ever closer and on 25 October, the Russians struck.

At 05:00 hours a large body of Russian troops was seen approaching the Allied positions from the east. The defences on that side consisted of an outer line of six redoubts erected on the Causeway Heights and an inner line to the north of Balaklava held by the Royal Marines (Marine Heights) with the 93rd Highlanders by the village of Kadikoi which guarded the exit from the harbour. Sir Colin Campbell was placed in charge of the defence of Balaklava.

The main Russian force was led by General Liprandi. His objective was to capture the Causeway Heights and then Kadikoi, and thus cutting British communications with Balaklava.

The Russians opened the fighting with a cannonade of No.1 Redoubt on what was called Canrobert's Hill at the rear of the Causeway Heights which dominated the South Valley and the ground towards Kadikoi.

The Cavalry Division was amongst the first to respond to the Russian attack and Lord Lucan attempted to harass the enemy as they approached. Sergeant George Cruse of the 1st Dragoons of Lieutenant General Scarlett's Heavy Brigade related the events of that initial cannonade. 'The Russian guns began to advance and several round shot fell into [our] ranks, breaking the legs of two Horses and one large ball struck a man named Middleton right in the face, of course killing him instantly ... they opened such a fire upon us that we could do nothing but retire which we did half a mile behind our encampment. Our tents had in the meantime been struck but because of the confusion they could not be packed up and we had the pleasure of galloping over all our little property.'[1]

Raglan had galloped up to his vantage point on the Sapouné Heights that marked the western limit of the Causeway Heights. From there he could see down into both the North Valley and the South Valley. What he saw from there was the Turkish defenders of the redoubts on the Causeway Heights being driven off by the Russians. Raglan could not allow the Russians to control the Causeway Heights and he ordered the 1st and 4th Divisions to retake the redoubts. This, though, would take time, especially as the 4th Division had just returned from a night in the siege trenches and the men were tired and cold.

The sluggish British response gave Liprandi his chance. Leading the Russian advance was a mixed force of 3,000 hussars and Cossacks. All that stood between them and Balaklava was the withdrawn Cavalry Division and the 93rd Highlanders of Sir Colin Campbell's Highland Brigade.

The Russian cavalry commander, Ryzhov, detached the 400-strong Ingermanland Hussars. As the Russian hussars bore down upon the lone battalion, the Highlanders waited quietly for the order to open fire. 'Not a man stirred,' wrote Fanny Duberly who had rushed up to the scene of the action from Balaklava, 'they stood like rocks till the Russian horses came to within about thirty yards – Then one terrific volley.'[12] In fact the Highlanders opened fire at probably about 800 yards, the maximum effective range of the Minié rifle. The Russians continued to charge forwards and the Highlanders replied with a second volley at around 500 yards.

The second volley caused the Russians to swerve to the Highlanders' right and some of the Scots showed signs of wanting to rush at the cavalry. Campbell shouted angrily, 'Ninety-Third! Ninety-Third! Damn all that eagerness!'[13]

To counter the Russian move towards the right, Campbell ordered the Grenadier Company to wheel round and fire upon the enemy cavalry. This was enough for the Russians, and they galloped back towards their main body, the cheers of the Highlanders ringing in their ears.

The immediate threat to Balaklava had been eliminated but the main mass of the Russian cavalry, at least 2,000 strong, crossed the Causeway Heights and headed down into the South Valley. Raglan had ordered the Heavy Brigade to go to the assistance of the 93rd and now it was the turn of Scarlett's men to tackle the Russian cavalry.

In the Heavy Brigade's front were two squadrons of the 2nd Royal North British Regiment of Dragoons (the Royal Scots Greys) and one squadron of the 6th (Inniskilling) Dragoons, just 300 men. At the appearance of the British, the Russians halted and extended their flanks. Scarlett simply charged straight at them.

'This charge was out and out the most exciting I ever saw or shall see again,' wrote Major Nigel Kingscote who was watching the battle unfold with Raglan from the Sapouné Heights. 'Being on high ground and close by one could see the fellows coming hand to hand blows beautifully, and our fellows did not spare them. We had to charge up hill and had not room to get our men into a swing or we should have shaken them still more. The Greys did their work well, so they all did, but the Greys looked beautiful.'[14]

The Scots Greys and the Inniskillings were enveloped by the Russians but at that moment the 5th Dragoon Guards crashed into the enemy. The opposing cavalry slashed and stabbed at each other.

'It was rather hot work for a few minutes,' remembered Sergeant Major Henry Franks of the 5th Dragoon Guards, 'there was no time to look about you. We soon became a struggling mass of half frenzied and desperate men, doing our level best to kill each other.' In the midst of the fighting, 27-year-old Sergeant Ramage of the Scots Greys rushed to the assistance of a private who was surrounded by seven Russians. Ramage drove them all off and saved the private's life. He was awarded the Victoria Cross.[15]

Among the men who charged with the 5th Dragoon Guards was Corporal Joseph Gough: 'We had no infantry up at the time, except the highlanders, who formed squares [sic], and popped them [the Russians] off nicely, so they retired from them. In the meantime, another lot of cavalry came to attack us. I suppose they thought we should run. At first we thought they were our Light Brigade till they got about twenty yards from us; then we saw the difference.

'We wheeled into line. They stood still, and we did not know what to do. The charge sounded and away we went into the midst of them. Such cutting and slashing for about a minute, it was dreadful to see; the rally sounded, but it was no use – none of us would come away till the enemy retreated; then our fellows cheered as loud as ever they could. When we were in the midst of them my horse was shot; he fell, and got up again, and I was entangled in the saddle; my head and one leg were on the ground. He tried to gallop on with the rest, but fell again, and I managed to get loose. While I was in that predicament a Russian lancer was going to run me through, and I could not help myself. Macnamara came up at the time, and nearly severed his head from his body; so, thank God, I did not get a scratch. I got up, and ran to where I saw a lot of loose horses; I got one belonging to one of the Enniskillens [6th Dragoons], and soon was along with the regiment again.'[16] Private Michael Gough was later awarded the newly instituted Distinguished Conduct Medal.

Next into the fray against the Russian's western flank charged the 4th (Royal Irish) Dragoon Guards followed by the 1st Royal Dragoons. The arrival of these two regiments proved too much for the Russians. 'The Russians stood for a few minutes,' wrote Major (later Lieutenant Colonel) Forrest of the 4th Dragoon Guards, 'and then retired precipitately but reformed in good order on top of a hill; but on getting one shot from our Horse Artillery, away they went. Lord Raglan, who by this time had arrived on the heights in our rear, sent an Aide de Camp with this message, "Well done the Heavy Brigade".'[17]

'View of the lines of Balaklava from Guard's Hill, Canrobert's Hill in the distance, the sirocco blowing,' was the caption for this photograph. When Fenton took this shot he recorded that the temperature was 82 degrees in the shade. The date was 26 March 1855. After just an hour's work his camera slides warped and split.

The camp of Captain, later Major Brandling's 'C' Troop of the Royal Horse Artillery shown here at its encampment near Kadikoi during the siege of Sevastopol. Brandling's troop of nine-pounder guns was one of those that engaged the Russian artillery on the Bulganek. He was later commended by Lord Lucan for his handling of his troop at the Battle of the Alma. On the morning of the Battle of Balaklava 'C' Troop had just returned from a daybreak parade at Inkerman, when the orders for reinforcements arrived. Captain Brandling made all speed with his guns, and reached the right rear of the Heavy Brigade as it was advancing to the charge. They unlimbered and came into action, firing on the Russian cavalry at a range of 700 or 800 yards, preventing all attempts by the enemy to rally. At the outset of the campaign the artillery consisted of two troops of horse artillery and eight field batteries.

The cavalry camp looking towards Kadikoi. This is a view eastwards; Balaklava is to the right and rear of this position.

Fenton described this photograph as the 'encampment of the 71st Regiment at Balaklava commissariat camp, Tents and huts of British camps on hillside and valley at Balaklava.' The limitations of Balaklava harbour and the difficulty it posed for its defence led to Raglan suggesting that all the British army's supplies, along with those of the French, could be drawn through the Kamiesh or Kazach. It was only when Commissary-General William Filder declared that if such a move took place he would be unable to feed the army, that Raglan accepted he would have to remain at Balaklava.

Commissary-General William Filder was heavily criticised for failings in the supply situation during the war, though he received unqualified support from Raglan, whom he described as 'an able man, and labours from Morning to Night, but his department is weak in numbers, and deficient in Field experience, and he is surrounded with difficulties'. On 21 July 1855, it was announced that a Medical Board had pronounced him unfit to continue with his command and he was forced to return to the UK. After the war Filder and a number of other officers demanded a board of inquiry into the experiences of the army in the Crimea. The report of the board largely exonerated those considered responsible for the terrible conditions the troops had to endure and was consequently labelled the 'Whitewashing Board'.

Brevet-Major Adolphus William Desart Burton and twelve officers of the 5th Dragoon Guards at camp. From left to right: are Major Burton; Dr Cattell; Lieutenant Montgomery; Lieutenant Hampton; Lieutenant Ferguson; Major Inglis; Captain Godman; Captain Halford; Lieutenant Burnand; and Quartermaster Bewley.

Another photograph of Adolphus Burton, this time in more formal attire. He is wearing his scarlet coatee with blue undress trousers which have a red stripe down the outside leg. He also has the white undress cross belt and waist belt. His headdress is the 'Albert' helmet without the usual black horsehair plume. Note the regimental number on the end of the round valise behind the saddle. Captain Burton commanded two squadrons of his regiment at the Battle of Balaklava. Burton tried to sell his commission so that he could return to Britain but was unable to raise more than the regulation price and so he remained with his regiment.

The Cavalry camp near Balaklava. The photograph shows the South Valley and beyond the Causeway Heights. It is easy to understand why the Causeway Heights were considered to be of supreme importance to both sides. If the Russians were able to establish themselves on the heights they would be able to dominate the British positions around Balaklava. The Battle of Balaklava was effectively a battle for control of the Causeway Heights.

This is a photograph of the Woronzov Road which ran along the top of the Causeway heights. The road ran directly into Sevastopol. The Causeway Heights were seized by the Russians early in the Battle of Balaklava. This particular part of the Woronzov Road is that at what was called the Victoria Ravine which marked the boundary between the French and the British lines. *(Imperial War Museum; Q71421)*

Watching events from alongside Raglan was Lieutenant Frederick Maxse, Royal Navy, who was his naval aide-de-camp. When Maxse saw the Turks abandoning the redoubts, he complained that they ran like 'cowardly curs at *first shot*, leaving *our* guns for the Russians to capture'. Maxse was formerly on the ninety-one gun screw battleship HMS *Agamemnon*.

Another image of Sir Colin Campbell. When the Russian cavalry bore down on the Highlanders, Colin Campbell rode along the front of the 93rd, telling the regiment to be steady and warning them that, if necessary, every man should have '"to die where he stood". He was answered by a universal and cheery response, "Ay, ay Sir Colin; we'll do that".'

Colonel Clarke of the Scots Greys (2nd Dragoons) shown here with his horse that was wounded at Balaklava. George Calvert Clarke was born in 1814 and was commissioned into an infantry regiment in 1834. He served in the West Indies, was promoted to lieutenant and then captain, and in 1848 he transferred to the Royal Scots Greys. When the war with Russia began, he was a Brevet Major. At the beginning of the battle Colonel H.D. Griffiths who commanded the Scots Greys, was wounded, stunned by a shot from a Russian marksman, and Brevet Major Clarke led his regiment into the attack. Note the hindquarters of his horse which has been branded 2D.

Lieutenant Temple Godman was the Adjutant of the 5th Dragoon Guards, shown here with his horse Earl and his servant, Kilburn. 'The enemy seemed quite astonished,' remarked Godman recalling the moment that the Russians realised that the Heavy Brigade was about to attack them, 'and drew into a walk and then a halt; as soon as they met, all I saw was swords in the air in every direction, the pistols going off, and everyone hacking away right and left.' This photograph was taken in March 1855 and afterwards he told his father that, 'I will tell you where to go in London for copies, as many as you please at 5s each'.

This image is listed as being Captain Bernard of the 5th Dragoon Guards, though this is possibly an error, being most probably Captain George Burnand. He suffered repeated sickness and missed the Battle of Balaklava through illness. In December 1854 Burnand told Temple Godman that 'he does not care to serve and wishes to get out of it soon, he says he can't stand another summer'. Eventually he handed his papers into the Horse Guards but because he had received his promotion to captain without purchase, he was only permitted to sell his other commissions. He, like Burton, therefore decided to stay with his regiment, much to the annoyance of those officers below him that hoped to succeed to his command of a troop.

Captain Charles Augustus Drake Halford, 5th Dragoon Guards. Drake Halford became a Cornet in the 5th Dragoon Guards on 30 March 1849, and rose to the rank of Lieutenant in April 1850 before being made a Captain on 8 December 1854 without purchase, being described by Temple Godman as 'a very good officer'.

Group of the 4th Dragoon Guards. Kinglake wrote that the men of the 4th Dragoon Guards had been advancing with their swords in their scabbards but at sight of a combat going on, though they were still hundreds of yards away, the men 'instinctively' drew their swords.

Captain John MacDonnell Webb (4th Dragoon Guards) standing in the doorway of his hut looking at Colonel Hodge (standing in profile), Mrs Rogers, Webb's servant with a horse, and several others of the 4th Dragoon Guards. Edward Cooper Hodge was commanding officer of the 4th Dragoon Guards from October 1848 to August 1859 and Colonel of the regiment from January 1874 until his death on 11 December 1894. He was a short man, nick-named 'Little Hodge' but he was liked by his men. The army suffered terribly in the Crimea even before hostilities began for the heavy cavalry. The 4th and 5th Dragoon Guards were at Varna for two months during which time cholera had so decimated the men that the two regiments were combined under Hodge's command. Of this photograph Hodge wrote home: 'I hope you will receive the photographic views of my hut and camp all safe … We are standing at the door of Webb's hut.'

Chapter Five

The Charge of the Light Brigade

The Light Brigade had been standing to since dawn on the day of the Battle of Balaklava and most of the men had not eaten that day. Neither had they had the chance to show their mettle and Cardigan and his officers seethed with frustration. The apparent reluctance of the Russians to advance further, following the precipitous withdrawal of their cavalry, however, prompted Raglan to mount a counter-attack and this would, at last, give the Light Division their chance.

Raglan had ordered the 1st Division and the 4th Division to recapture the redoubts, the first three of which appeared to be only lightly held. The cavalry was also to play its part. An order was sent to Lucan with the following instructions: 'Cavalry to advance and take advantage of any opportunity to recover the heights. They will be supported by the infantry which have been ordered [to] advance on two fronts.'[18]

Lucan understood this instruction to mean that he should wait until the infantry arrived before making any moves against the redoubts. Indeed, it would have been unwise to have mounted an attack without infantry support.

As Raglan waited on the heights for his counter-attack to develop it appeared that the Russians were preparing to remove the guns from the redoubts. If the Russians were able to capture a considerable number of guns they would be able to claim a victory. This could not be allowed to happen but with the infantry still some distance away only the cavalry would be able to reach the redoubts in time.

So Captain Nolan, one of Raglan's aides, was summoned to take a message to Lord Lucan. Nolan rushed down the slope from Raglan's position and galloped up to Lucan. After handing over Raglan's order, the captain and the general spoke for a few moments. Lucan then rode over to Lord Cardigan.

According to Cardigan, Lucan 'came in front of the Brigade, ordered the 11th Hussars to fall back in support and told me to attack the Russian guns in the Valley, about three quarters of a mile distant with the 13th Lt. Dragoons & 17th Lancers. I answered "Certainly but allow me to point out to you that the hills on each side are covered with Artillery & Riflemen." The Lt. General replied "I cannot help it, you must attack, Lord Raglan desires the Lt. Brigade immediately to attack the enemy".[19]

From where Lucan and Cardigan were sitting on their horses they could not see what was happening in the redoubts above. The only guns they could see were those pointing down from the Fedioukine Heights and the 3rd Don Cossack battery formed up at the head of the North Valley in front of them. The latter, it seemed, was what Raglan was referring to.

Cardigan rode to the head of his brigade. He told Colonel George Paget to take command of the second line and ordered the brigade to draw swords. Beginning at a walk, with the first squadron of the 17th Lancers leading the way, the light cavalry started off down the valley.

The Fedioukine heights to the left of the advancing Light Brigade were still held by General Zhaboritski with at least eight battalions of infantry, four squadrons of cavalry and fourteen pieces of artillery. Ahead, the 3rd Don Cossack battery was supported in the rear by the main Russian cavalry force. Though the standard number of guns in a Russian battery was eight, some believe that a battery and a half was present, totalling at least twelve guns. Against this considerable force rode 650 men of the Light Brigade.

At this point Captain Nolan, who had asked Cardigan if he could join the brigade in the attack, realised that a terrible mistake had been made and that instead of moving to stop the artillery being removed from the redoubts, the Light Brigade was heading towards a fully-formed battery along a valley bristling with thousands of enemy troops. Nolan was seen to gallop ahead of Cardigan to try and prevent disaster but was struck and killed by a cannonball from one of the guns on the Fedioukine Heights.

Onward rode the Light Brigade, into the Valley of Death, now under continuous rifle and artillery fire from the heights on their left flank. The guns of the Don Cossack battery also began to fire upon the advancing cavalry, as William Russell of the *London Illustrated News*, graphically described: 'At the distance of 1,200 yards the whole line of the enemy belched forth, from thirty iron mouths, a flood of smoke and flame, through which hissed the deadly balls. Their flight was marked by instant gaps in our ranks, by dead men and horses, by steeds flying wounded or rider-less across the plain.'

First with round shot and then case shot as the Light Brigade moved ever closer, increasing its pace to a gallop, the Don Cossacks could hardly miss. 'It thinned us like sickle through grass,' wrote one survivor, and the precise order of the ranks was disrupted as the gunfire brought down dozens of men and horses. Although the officers did their best to keep formation, increasingly the men had to ride around men and horses lying dead or injured on the ground. Soon the 8th Hussars had broken away from the rest of the brigade, disappearing into the smoke and dust.

As the Light Brigade charged towards the head of the valley, four squadrons of the *Chasseurs d'Afrique* were sent against the batteries on the Fedioukine Heights. General Morris, in command of the two French cavalry brigades, had drawn up the *Chasseurs d'Afrique* about half a mile to the north of the British cavalry's original position and these now advanced up the slope of the heights, driving in the Russian skirmishers who joined the rest of the infantry which formed square as the cavalry approached. The Russian artillery, though, was left exposed and the *Chasseurs* were soon amongst the gunners. Some of the gunners were able to limber up their guns and retreat but many were cut down. General Zhaboritski ordered a counter-attack by the Vladimir Infantry Regiment which marched along the heights. The *Chasseurs* were now widely dispersed and under fire from the Russian squares and, with the Vladimir Regiment approaching, the recall was sounded. The *Chasseurs* retired in good order having effectively silenced the batteries on the Fedioukine heights. It cost them ten men killed and twenty-eight wounded.

Lucan had also ordered the Heavy Brigade to support the Light Brigade but as the Heavies came under fire from the Fedioukine Heights (Lucan himself being slightly wounded) and when he saw what was happening ahead to the light cavalry, he reined back, and with the words 'They have sacrificed the Light Brigade; they shall not have the Heavy if I can help it', he led Scarlett's men back along the valley, intending to cover the Light Brigade's withdrawal.[20]

Nothing, though, could stop the Light Brigade with Cardigan still proudly at its head and its momentum took it through the hail of gunfire and into the Russian battery. 'The first line was broken – it was joined by the second, they never halted or checked their speed an instant,' continued Russell. 'With diminished ranks, thinned by those thirty guns, which the Russians had laid with the most deadly accuracy, with a halo of flashing steel above their heads, and with a cheer which was many a noble fellow's death cry, they flew into the smoke of the batteries; but ere they were lost from view, the plain was strewed with their bodies and with the carcasses of horses. They were exposed to an oblique fire from the batteries on the hills on both sides, as well as to a direct fire of musketry.

'Through the clouds of smoke we could see their sabers [*sic*] flashing as they rode up to the guns and dashed between them, cutting down the gunners as they stood.' Incredibly, the Light Brigade had ridden through the storm of shot and at last could give vent to its fury. The men stabbed with their lances and hacked with their swords at those who had inflicted such carnage upon their comrades. The Russian gunners were killed by their guns or cut down as they tried to run.

Behind the battery was the main body of the Russian cavalry and General Ryzhov sent his lightly-armed Cossacks to engage the Light Brigade. But at the sight of the British cavalry tearing towards them, they turned and fled the way they had come pushing past their own cavalry, even using their swords on their countrymen to escape. The Kievsky and Ingermanland regiments were thrown back on each other with the impact of the British charge, which had scarcely lost its impetus even though it had to negotiate the Russian guns. The Hussars, Lancers and Light Dragoons hacked and slashed at the Russian cavalry, driving it back towards the river and its own transport lines.

Though they had overrun the battery and caused mayhem amongst the Russian cavalry regiments, the Light Brigade was now dispersed around the head of the valley and was in danger of being annihilated unless it could be rallied and reformed. Cardigan had led the brigade well in the charge but he no longer possessed any degree of control, and seemed at a loss as what to do next. Other officers were trying to gather their men together.

Paget, being at the head of the second line, was able to stop many of his men rushing towards the Russian cavalry. He did all he could to disable as many Russian guns as possible and then, assembling around sixty or seventy men, mostly from the 4th Light Dragoons and 11th Hussars, he began to withdraw.

In the confusion of the charge and the poor visibility the 8th Hussars missed the guns altogether, coming to a halt a few hundred yards beyond. All that Colonel Shewell, in command of the Hussar Brigade, could see was the Russian cavalry ahead and he prepared to attack them when he was informed that other elements of the Russian cavalry had ridden down from the Causeway and cut off the Light Brigade's retreat. Realising the seriousness of the situation, Shewell wheeled his men round and retired back along the valley.

As the 8th Hussars retreated they found that their path was indeed blocked by the Russian Uhlans. 'Colonel Shewell, of the 8th Hussars, saw the danger, and rode his few men straight at them, cutting his way through with fearful loss,' reported William Russell. 'The other regiments turned and engaged in a desperate encounter. With courage too great almost for credence, they were breaking their way through the columns which enveloped them, when there took place an act of atrocity without parallel in the modern warfare of civilized nations. The Russian gunners, when the storm of cavalry passed, returned to their guns. They saw their own cavalry mingled with the troopers who had just ridden over them, and to the eternal disgrace of the Russian name the miscreants poured a murderous volley of grape and canister on the mass of struggling men and horses, mingling friend and foe in one common ruin.'

Mrs Fanny Duberly accompanied her husband, Captain Henry Duberly the Paymaster of the 8th Hussars, to the Crimea and her collected letters and journal were published in 1855. She was the only British woman at the front line and despite Lord Raglan's disapproval, she remained there until the end of the war. Of the Charge of the Light Brigade she wrote: 'Now came the disaster of the day – our glorious and fatal charge ... Advancing by themselves, although in the face of the whole Russian force, and under a fire that seemed pouring from all sides, as though every bush was a musket, every stone in the hillside a gun. Faster and faster they rode. How we watched them! They are out of sight; but presently come a few horsemen, straggling, galloping back. "What can those *skirmishers* be doing? See, they form up together again. Good! God! It is the Light Brigade!"

'At five o'clock that evening Henry and I turned, and rode up to where these men had formed up in the rear (& shook hands with them — poor fellows our hearts were all too full for many words).

'Past the scene of the morning we rode slowly; round us were dead and dying horses, numberless; and near me lay a Russian soldier, very still, upon his face. In a vineyard a little to my right a Turkish soldier was also stretched out dead. The horses, mostly dead, were all unsaddled, and the attitudes of some betokened extreme pain.'

Of the approximately 650 men that charged into the Valley of Death, 118 were killed, 127 wounded and about sixty taken prisoner (numbers vary slightly). After regrouping, only 195 men were still with horses, of which 335 or more were also killed or put down afterwards. Many of the wounded men later died in the squalid Turkish hospitals. Though the reputation of the British cavalry had been greatly enhanced, the Russians saw the Battle of Balaklava as a victory. They had captured the British redoubts and captured seven artillery pieces which were taken back to Sevastopol as trophies. More importantly Raglan decided not to attempt to regain the Causeway Heights, which meant that the Allies were confined to a narrow area between Balaklava and Sevastopol. It also encouraged the Russians into believing that they could beat the Allies and plans were soon formed to attack the Allied positions again and drive the invaders back to their ships.

'Captain Portal, 4th Light Dragoons equipped for Balaklava'. Robert Portal wrote a letter home about this photograph, and others of the 4th Light Dragoons: 'Mr Fenton has made several sketches of our camp, and whenever he goes home you must get some of them, the numbers are No. 7, Captain Portal and servant in marching order, before Balaklava Charge. No. 10, Captain P. and servant in a winter dress going on picket. Nos. 18 and 19 Views of the 4th Light Dragoons' camp, which were very good indeed'. Below is one of those photos, this one being labelled 'Camp of the 4th Light Dragoons, soldiers quarters'.

Situated between the Fedioukine Heights and the Causeway, was the North Valley, and thanks to Tennyson's poem it became known as 'The Valley of Death'. Fenton took two photographs here, one of which was without the cannonballs dispersed along the road, leading to speculation that he arranged for them to be placed there to create a more dramatic effect. However, when Fenton visited there on 4 April 1855, he wrote in a private letter, 'the sight passed all imagination: round shot and shell lay like a stream at the bottom of the hollow all the way down, you could not walk without treading upon them'. All this is academic, however, as this does not appear to be the ground over which the Light Brigade charged.

Second Lieutenant M.V. Yates of the 11th Hussars. Yates was made adjutant one month before the Battle of Balaklava but he did not take part in the charge due to temporary illness. He retired as a Captain on half pay in 1859 and died in July 1862.

Colonel Doherty and men of the 13th Light Dragoons, including Cornet Danzil Chamberlain, Captain Jenyns and veterinary-surgeon Thomas Towers. Vet Towers took part in the charge as did Chamberlain who had his horse shot under him. The 13th Light Dragoons formed the first line of the Light Brigade on the right of the 17th Lancers. The 13th Light Dragoons lost three officers in the charge (Captains Oldham and Goad and Cornet Montgomery), and eleven other ranks. Thirty-two men were wounded and another ten were taken prisoner. Amongst the survivors of the charge was Sergeant Joseph Malone, of the 13th Light Dragoons 'E' Troop. His horse had been killed in the charge and he was returning back up the valley when he saw Troop Sergeant-Major John Berryman, trying to move a severely wounded officer. Though still under very heavy fire, Malone stopped and helped the other two NCOs carry the officer out of range of the Russian guns. For his actions that day Malone was awarded the Victoria Cross.

Colonel Shewell was in command of the Hussar Brigade and was with the 8th Hussars that formed the second line alongside Paget and the 4th Light Dragoons during the charge. Shewell had actually been lying ill in Balaklava on the morning of the battle but when he heard about the Russian attack he got up from his sick bed and hurried to join his regiment, arriving just in time to lead them in the charge. He was seen by Fanny Duberly shortly after the battle: 'Colonel Shewell came up to me, looking flushed, and conscious of having fought like a brave and gallant soldier, and having earned his laurels well.'

Cornet Henry John Wilkin, 11th Hussars. On 2 February 1855, Assistant Surgeon Wilkins purchased the rank of cornet in the 11th Hussars, and is photographed here in full hussar dress of the 11th (or Prince Albert's Own) Hussars. This uniform consisted of a brown fur busby with a crimson bag. The horsehair plume was white over crimson. The blue tunic had horizontal yellow frogging (gold for officers). The trousers or overalls were crimson with a double yellow, or gold, vertical stripe. The barrelled sash was of yellow/gold over crimson worsted cord. The sword belt was white. Lord Cardigan was the 11th's colonel.

Captain Edward Phillips and Lieutenant Yates, 8th Hussars. The 8th Hussars were in the second line on the left of the 4th Light Dragoons. The regiment's correct title at the time was 8th (The King's Royal Irish) Regiment of (Light) Dragoons (Hussars). Phillips, a lieutenant at the time of the charge, had his horse shot from under him, surrounded by Russian lancers. The Russians were recalled and Phillips was able to make his way back to the British lines, riding bareback on a rider-less horse because he could not twist its slipped saddle back into position.

Lieutenant King, 4th Light Dragoons. Born in 1830 as the son of Vice-Admiral Sir Richard King, and holding the rank of Cornet, William Affleck King was twenty-four years old at the time of the Battle of Balaklava. He survived the charge unwounded and later rose to the rank of Major in the 17th Regiment.

Captain (Brevet-Major) Brown, 4th Light Dragoons and servant in winter dress. As the brigade advanced Paget could hear Brown shouting, 'Close in to your centre back the right flank; keep up, Private So-and-so. Left squadron keep back; look to your dressing.' These were sounds, Paget remarked, that were familiar on the parade ground, 'but hardly perhaps to be expected on such a job as ours, and showing how impervious they were to all that was going on around them, and how impossible it was for them, even under such circumstances, to forget the rules of parade, but which perhaps had the effect of checking the unusual pace at which the first line was leading us.' George John Brown was one of 746 British soldiers awarded the *Légion d'Honneur* by the French for their service in the Crimea.

Brigadier-General Lord George Paget CB. On 17 August 1840, Paget purchased an unattached company, and exchanged to a troop in the 4th Light Dragoons. He became a Major on 30 January 1846, and then Lieutenant-Colonel on 29 December. By the time his regiment sailed for the Crimea, Paget was a Brevet-Colonel and the most senior officer in the Light Brigade after Lord Cardigan. 'Lord George led our line gallantly,' wrote Private Connor of the 4th Light Dragoons. 'There was no sign of flinching; but he made us laugh as he kept drawling out in his own peculiar tone, "Now then men, come on".' When Cardigan left the Crimea, Paget assumed command of the Light Brigade. After a brief period in Britain following the death of his father, Paget returned to the Crimea and resumed his command of the Light Brigade. He also took temporary command of the Cavalry Division in the absence of Brigadier-General Scarlett.

Two Sergeants of the 4th Light Dragoons. One of their men, Private Griggs recalled the moment when the 4th Light Dragoons reached the Don Cossack battery and he rode at one of the mounted Russian drivers: 'He cut me across the eyes with his whip, which almost blinded me, but as my horse flew past I made a cut and caught him in the mouth, so that his teeth all rattled together as he fell. I can hear the horrible sound now.'

'Colonel Lowe (or Low), 4th Light Dragoons and servant in winter dress.' Alexander Low was still a captain in the Crimea and at the time of the Charge of the Light Brigade in which he reputedly played a significant part. Low allegedly accounted for thirteen Russian gunners and was described by a fellow officer as being 'a fine figure of a man, weighing fifteen stone – a most gallant fellow – and perhaps the best cavalry officer in the service'. He became Colonel of his regiment in 1881.

'Group of officers, the 8th Hussars.' From left to right in this photo is Regimental Sergeant-Major Harding, Quartermaster Lane in a sheepskin coat and Paymaster Henry Duberly. The mounted officer is Captain Lord Killeen. The group on the other side includes Sergeant-Major Clarke and Sergeant O'Meara who also feature in the photograph of the 8th Hussars' cookhouse. The officer reading a paper is Captain Phillips. Standing next to Phillips is Doctor Anderson. The seated figures in the middle of this group are, again from the left, Sergeant-Major Williams, and in front of him is Cornet William Mussenden. Mussenden rose through the ranks, becoming Colonel of the regiment in 1874, eventually reaching the rank of Major-General. Half hidden, next to Mussenden is Lieutenant (later Captain and Brevet-Major) Clement Walker Heneage who received the Victoria Cross during the Indian Mutiny. Standing next to him is Captain Edward Tomkinson.

The title given to this photograph by Fenton is simply: 'Mounted soldier, the pocket-pistol – equipped for Balaklava.' Though the soldier appears to be a member of the 4th Light Dragoons, as the number on his valise seems to bear the number IV, his uniform is clearly that of the 13th Light Dragoons. This can be determined by the fact that the collar and cuffs of his jacket are yellow, whereas those of the 4th Light Dragoons was scarlet. This is further emphasized by the broad stripe down his blue overalls, which is obviously not scarlet. Other images of the two light dragoon regiments at this time support this view. The only conclusion to be drawn from this is that his valise is upside down and that the number, which can only be partially seen, is actually XIII.

Quartermaster John Hill of the 4th Light Dragoons. Though Hill was in an administrative role he did take part in the charge. It would seem possible that the charger on which he sits in this photograph was the one he rode into the battle as the horse carries visible scars. Note the forage cap that Hill is wearing. Although the distinguishing regimental colours of the 4th Light Dragoons was scarlet, the forage cap had a yellow band. That of the 13th Light Dragoons, confusingly, was white.

Cooking house of the 8th Hussars. Of the 293 other ranks who had set out for the Crimea with the 8th Hussars, two were promoted to officer rank, forty-two were invalided, sixty-eight died of wounds or disease, twenty-six were killed in action or died immediately afterwards. One private deserted to the Russians. Of those that were lost from the 8th Hussars was Lieutenant Lord John Fitzgibbon. 'I saw Lord Fitzgibbon, who was mortally wounded, pull out his purse and offer it to anyone of us who would dismount and accept it, as he did not like it to get into the hands of the Russians,' remembered Trooper Sheridan, 'but Lord! We did not think of money as such a moment as that. Life and honour were more precious to us than money, so I suppose the Russians got the English gold after all.' Just visible to the left of the photograph is Roger Fenton's photographic van.

Captain George, 4th Light Dragoons, and servant. Though George was the regiment's paymaster he took part in the charge. One of the 4th Light Dragoon privates, recalled the moment they galloped up to the Don Cossack Battery, 'as soon as we reached the guns the men began dodging by getting under them, and for a time defended themselves with rammers; but it was no contest – they had no chance with us and we cut them down like ninepins.'

A group of men and an officer of the *Chasseurs d'Afrique*. 'The gallant conduct of the *Chasseurs d'Afrique* deserves especial mention,' recalled Major Adye. 'Formed on the left of the light cavalry, as the latter advanced to the charge, the *Chasseurs* rushed upon the artillery of the enemy stationed on the Fedioukine Heights, turned their flank, and put their gunners to sword; thus making an important diversion in which they suffered severely.' The *Chasseurs* wore a light blue tunic with yellow facings. The trousers were red. Their headgear was a light blue and red shako called a *taconnet*.

Fenton also described this photograh as one of an officer of the *Chasseurs d'Afrique* and others have stated that this was a French infantry officer; French sources call the individual shown here an *Officier du Train*.

Mrs Duberly wrote about this photograph in one of her letters home on 14 April 1855: 'Henry's beard will astonish you – the old brute knew he was going to have his picture taken – and stood all no how on purpose to spite me.' Nevertheless, this particular photograph sold remarkably well. Fanny Duberly applied for a medal for being present at the Battle of Balaklava and received considerable support in this from senior officers. Her reasoning for this was that she was almost captured by the Russians. She had ridden up from the harbour as the Russian cavalry swept over the Fedioukine Heights. 'Looking on the crest of the nearest hill, I saw it covered with running Turks, pursued by mounted Cossacks, who were making straight for where I stood, striking our tent and packing our valuables,' Mrs Duberly wrote. 'Henry flung me on the old horse; and seizing a pair of laden saddle-bags, a great coat, and a few other loose packages, I made my way over a ditch into a vineyard ... Henry joined me just in time to ride a little to the left, to get clear of the shots, which now began to fly towards us'.

Chapter Six

The Battle of Inkerman

After the excitement of the events of 25 October the siege of Sevastopol settled back into its dreary, but hazardous routine. The morning of 5 November 1854 was not much different than those that had preceded it though it had been a misty night and as dawn approached the mist turned into a heavy fog. Visibility had become so poor that Major Goodwyn had withdrawn his pickets of the 2nd Division's 41st Regiment from the top of Shell Hill in the belief that in foggy weather 'the enemy would be better observed on the skyline from the base than from the top of the hill'.

So wet and miserable were the men on picket duty that when the relieving troops arrived an hour before dawn, the usual practice of both bodies remaining in place until daybreak was dispensed with. The tired and cold troops trudged off to camp as the sky began to lighten.

In the valley below, hidden by the mist and camouflaged by their grey greatcoats, the soldiers of General Soimonov's army moved south-eastwards directly towards the 2nd Division.

The first shots of the Battle of Inkerman were fired by a body of sharpshooters under Goodlake of the Coldstream Guards of the 1st Division who saw columns of Russian infantry moving up the plateau towards Shell Hill. The gunfire alerted the Grenadier Company of the 41st Regiment commanded by Captain Hugh Rowlands, which formed the advanced pickets of the 2nd Division: 'I ran up to enquire the cause when one shouted out that there were columns of Russians close to them. I stood to my arms and advanced in extended order, thinking it was a sortie ... Getting on top of the hill I found myself close upon, very truly, thousands of Russians. I immediately gave an order to retire, which was done for about 200 yards, when I halted on the next bit of high ground and lay down waiting for them ...

'When we retired the Russians came on with the most fiendish yells you can imagine. We commenced firing. To my dismay, I found that half the firelocks missed fire, which dispirited the men. At this period the Russian columns opened with their field pieces, pouring in grape and shell. We then got some reinforcements from the 55th and the 30th but were gradually obliged to retire. I begged and entreated Colonel Haly to allow me to charge, which he did. After a little hand-to-hand work we turned them and drove them back about 500 yards, when we were met by a fresh column and compelled to retire.'[21]

During this fighting Colonel Haly was wounded and dragged from his horse to the ground. Hugh Rowlands saw this and cut his way through the enemy to rescue the colonel helped by 22-year-old Private McDermond of the 47th Regiment who killed the Russian that had wounded Haly. The two men saved Colonel Haly and both were subsequently awarded the Victoria Cross.

The rest of the 2nd Division was now up and under arms. Sir George De Lacy Evans, the sixty-seven-year-old commander of the 2nd Division, was on a ship in Balaklava, recovering from his injuries after being thrown from his horse. Command had therefore devolved upon Brigadier-General Pennefather.

Pennefather decided to hold his ground as far forward as possible and wait to be reinforced rather than falling back upon the main British position. By this time Raglan had ridden up to see what was happening. Though he did not interfere with Pennefather, he saw that artillery was going to play a crucial part in the battle and he called up two 18-pounders from the Siege Train which could out-range the Russian field guns. These, though, had to be hauled two-and-a-half miles up to the Sandbag Battery and would not come into play for some time.

Nevertheless, Pennefather's men were holding their own and the other British divisions were moving up to Home Ridge. The situation appeared to be under control, or at least that was how it was perceived by George Brown and Lord Cathcart as when General Bosquet, in charge of a detached French force called the Corps of Observation, offered the help of infantry and artillery the two British generals informed him that they did not need his help. That situation, however, was about to change very dramatically as Soimonov launched his main attack.

With skirmishers deployed in front, twelve battalion columns, amounting to more than 9,000 men, headed for Home Ridge. Pauloff's 16,000-strong column, which had marched across Inkerman Bridge, and passed East Jut, also now began to move against The Barrier which was a wall the British had built to block the post road into Sevastopol. Pauloff's force was met by a wing of the 30th Regiment at the Barrier. Lieutenant Colonel Mauleverer ordered the 30th to fire a volley but most of these men had been on picket duty all night and a lot of their damp rifles misfired. Mauleverer, and the 30th's Adjutant, Lieutenant Walker, responded immediately by charging the Russians with the bayonet. The wing of the 30th, little more than 200 strong, drove 2,500 Russians back upon each other and the whole mass gave way and retreated. Walker received the Victoria Cross.

The next Russian onslaught was directed at the Sandbag Battery to the east of The Barrier. This was met by the 41st and 49th Regiments. The 41st held its ground, but the 49th was forced to give way but eventually made a stand.

The next British reinforcements now arrived on the scene in the form of the 1st Division. The Sandbag Battery had been seized by the Russians and the Duke of Cambridge sought to recover it. The British artillery now began to make its presence felt as the Grenadier Guards, just 700 strong, led the counter-attack against 7,000 Russians who formed a semi-circle around the battery. After a single volley the Grenadiers charged the Russians who abandoned the battery and fled down into the valley below.

Predictably, the Russians reformed and attempted to re-take the battery. Time and again the Russians tried to take the earthwork, and each time the Guards charged and drove their assailants back, as Grenadier Alfred Tipping described: 'After about three minutes to give the men breathing time we charged again but they were too many for us and would not move. Three of us got under the parapet and there they were with the muzzles of their guns close to our heads, but could not depress them sufficiently to shoot us and the moment their heads came over the top we had either a revolver or a sword to receive them with.' Eventually, however, the weight of the Russian attacks became too great for the Guards to withstand, and they withdrew. Incredibly, the Grenadiers refused to accept defeat and they once again charged the heights and took back the battery.[22]

Cathcart's 4th Division then arrived on the scene. Raglan ordered Cathcart to fill the gap that had developed between the Sandbag Battery and the Barrier. This opening, some 400 yards across, compromised the entire British defensive line but Cathcart believed that the greater threat came from the Selenghinsk Regiment which was bearing down on the British right flank. He disregarded Raglan's order and with six companies of the 46th and 68th Regiments he attacked the head of the Russian column – 'a dark mass of long brown and grey coats, flat caps and blue steel'.

Initially Cathcart's men pushed back the Russian column in some disorder. They were joined by Captain Burnaby who led a party of Grenadiers into the fray. Private Bancroft was with Burnaby, 'I bayoneted the first Russian in the chest; he fell dead. I was then stabbed in the mouth with great force, which caused me to stagger back, where I shot this second Russian and ran through a third. A fourth and fifth came at me and ran me through the side. I fell but managed to run one through and brought him down.'[23]

However, Cathcart had made a terrible mistake in rushing at the enemy as his own force was also in a highly disorganised state. The Russians regained their composure and were reforming whilst other Russians, including artillery fired down at the 68th and the 46th. Realising his error Cathcart was heard to mutter, 'I fear we are in a mess.' Cathcart took shelter behind some rocks but when he left their shelter to speak to Major Maitland he was shot through the chest.

The Duke of Cambridge, with the Grenadiers also found himself all but surrounded by the enemy. The Duke and his men had to cut their way through the Russian ranks ahead of them whilst a further two battalions moved against the Guards' flank. These battalions of the Okhotsk Regiment were distracted, however, by a doctor! Assistant-Surgeon Wolseley of the 20th Regiment had established his aid post in the Sandbag Battery. With the cry 'Fix bayonets, charge, and keep uphill.' He led a mixture of troops against the two Okhotsk battalions. Wolseley's group and the Guards managed to regain the British line, though they suffered heavy casualties in forcing their way through the Russian infantry.

It was at this stage of the battle when the French intervened, coming up from the rear to the British right. The appearance of Bosquet's Zouaves was greeted with cheers of 'Vive Francais' and the French soldiers replied with 'Vivent les Anglais!' and 'Vive l'Empereur' as they passed by and with typical élan, they overran the Sandbag Battery. The appearance of the French was the first of a series of events that began to turn the battle against the Russians. The next was the arrival of the 18-pounders that Raglan had called forward. Though the Russians had amassed nearly 100 guns on Shell Hill the 18-pounders were so much heavier that their shot smashed into the Russian batteries with devastating effect.

'I had only two 18-pounders with me,' wrote Colonel Collingwood Dickson, 'but as these were of heavier metal and superior calibre to the guns of the Russian field artillery, we were enabled not only to cope with them and to keep down their fire, but to overwhelm them wherever we directed their fire along their lines of batteries, and the superior range of our guns was such that they could not retire to any distance to keep out of the range of the 18-pounders without losing the power of returning our fire, and so we eventually compelled the Russians to withdraw their artillery from the field.'[24]

The Russians, though, were not finished. General Pauloff still had 6,000 men in hand and, forming them into eight battalion columns with four in reserve, he moved against Home Ridge in the centre of the British position. Pennefather had few troops not engaged to oppose them and the Russians overran three guns of Turner's battery and mounted Home Ridge. All that now stood between them and the camp of the 2nd Division and the Post Road was one French regiment, the 7th Léger. The French charged forward to meet the Russians but were driven back.

The 7th Léger rallied and with the help of the 55th, 57th and 77th regiments they stopped the Russians in their tracks. At that moment Colonel Daubeney ordered the 55th to charge. This inspired the 7th Léger and they too rushed at the Russians, bayonets levelled. Then the 63rd and the 21st struck the flank of the Russians.

The Russians were driven back and now was the moment for the Allies to seal the victory, or as Pennefather said to Raglan, 'Lick them to the Devil!' But Marshal Canrobert, who had now arrived on the British right with further reinforcements, would not agree to a general advance. The Russians had been defeated and that was enough.

Defeated, the Russians certainly were. Out of the 40,000 troops engaged, they had lost 10,729 men killed, wounded or taken prisoner, including six generals. The British had suffered 2,357 casualties but as Henry Clifford remarked, 'we are but ill able to stand such "Victories".'[25]

A panorama of the plateau of Sevastopol, looking towards the encampment of the Light Division, with Inkerman in the distance and the camp of the 2nd Division off to the right. Between the two camps was the Wellway.

A French redoubt on the Inkerman heights.

Twenty-two-years-old Brevet Major (later Lieutenant General) Gerald Littlehales Goodlake of the 1st Battalion Coldstream Guards held his position against large numbers of Russian infantry. His party killed thirty-eight of the attackers (including an officer) and took three prisoners. He was awarded the Victoria Cross. Goodlake had been involved in the thick of the fighting on 26 October when the Russians made a reconnaissance in force upon the Inkerman heights. In what was known as the Battle of Little Inkerman, Goodlake, carrying a rifle, was instrumental in holding off the Russians. Though the Russians were driven away, they had seen how lightly held the heights were and it encouraged them to mount the full-scale attack on 4 November.

Two photographs of the 47th Regiment. (*Above*) A group of the 47th Regiment in winter dress ready to go to take their turn in the trenches, just as they would have appeared in November 1854. (*Opposite*) Lieutenant John Sherwood Gaynor of the 47th. He died of fever on board HMS *Queen*, aged twenty-five, on 27 August 1855. At Inkerman a small band of the 47th became isolated by the fog from all the other combats going on around it. It was attacked by a huge Russian column, but its fire-power, in what was described as 'a classic line-verse-column battle,' the 47th stopped the Russians in their tracks and then drove them back almost to the foot of Shell Hill.

Brigadier-General Pennefather with a Light Dragoon orderly. Pennefather was praised for his bold handling of the battle. *'Ah! Quell brave garçon!'* exclaimed General Canrobert after the battle, *'quell brave homme! Quell bon general!'*

Lieutenant Mark Walker VC. According to his Victoria Cross citation during the fighting at the Barrier, Lieutenant Walker 'jumped over a wall in the face of two battalions of Russian Infantry which were marching towards it. This act was to encourage the men, by example, to advance against such odds – which they did and succeeded in driving back both battalions.' In spite of subsequently losing an arm during the first attack upon the Sevastopol Redan, Walker continued in the Army. He ended his 46-year army career as a general, receiving a knighthood in 1893, and died at Folkestone in 1902 at the age of 75.

Men of the 68th Regiment in winter dress. The 68th (Durham Light Infantry) was in the 1st Brigade of Cathcart's 4th Division. On the morning of the Battle of Inkerman, two companies of the 68th were returning from duty in the trenches in front of Sevastopol, being relieved by two other companies of the regiment, when the Russians attacked. Though the Crimea has a climate not unlike that of the Mediterranean, the winter of 1854/5 was the coldest in decades and the morning of 4 November was no exception. Naturally the 68th wore their grey greatcoats, as did the other regiments involved, and no doubt, if this photograph is any indication, whatever clothing they could acquire to keep themselves warm. When on guard duty the 68th used to wear their greatcoats over their accoutrements and that is how they were dressed when they set off towards the ridge and the advancing Russians. Of course dressed this way they could not reach their ammunition so before engaging the enemy the 68th had to halt and take off their greatcoats. As a consequence the 68th fought at Inkerman in red coats, the only regiment to do so.

Men of the 68th in their red coats, as they would have fought at Inkerman.

Major Stephen Remnant Chapman, 20th Regiment. The 20th had joined Cathcart's reckless advance and were forced to withdraw under persistent pressure from the Russians. Lieutenant Colonel Frederick Horn found himself with only about 150 men of the 20th and a few more from other regiments being attacked by two heavy Russian columns. The 20th were still armed with Brown Bess muskets at that stage of the war. An Assistant Engineer during the siege, Chapman was wounded on 8 September 1855 and died twelve days later. Buried on Cathcart's Hill, Chapman was thirty-years-old.

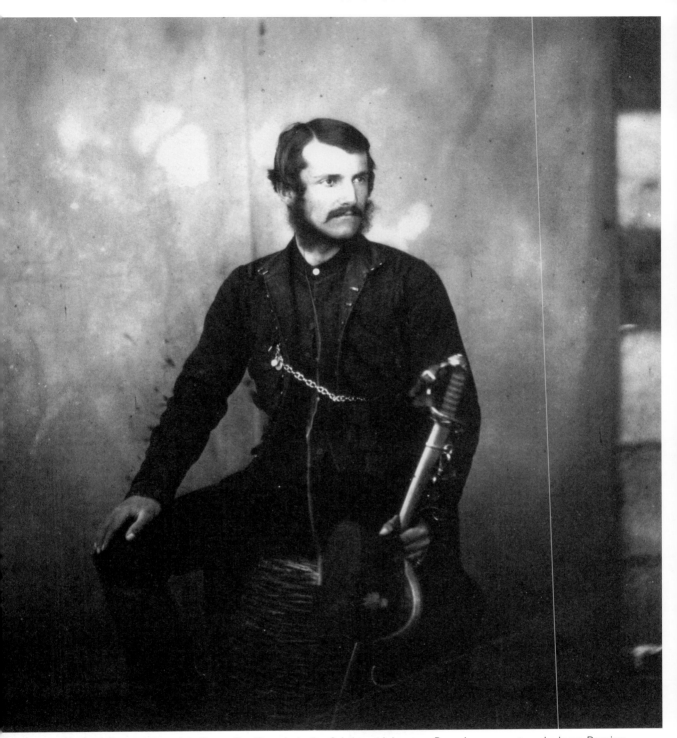

Captain Edwyn Sherard Burnaby, Grenadier Guards. In the fighting at Inkerman Burnaby encountered a huge Russian officer, as described by Kinglake: 'Upon seeing Burnaby, the Russian officer sprang at him sword in hand, but Burnaby parried; and before his assailant could again raise the arm, brought him down by a cut so delivered on the side of the head, that the tall leader fell, and died at once with a groan.' In October 1855 he was made Assistant Quartermaster General and he eventually became a Major General and MP for North Leicestershire.

Captain Sir Henry Hugh Clifford, of the Rifles, was General Buller's aide-de-camp. Clifford takes up the story as the 77th reached the top of the Wellway: 'I saw the enemy in great numbers in our front, about 15 yards from us; it was a moment or two before I could make General Buller believe that they were Russians. "In God's name," I said, "fix bayonets and charge!" He gave the order and in another moment we were hand-to-hand with them. Our line was not long enough to prevent the Russians out-flanking our left, which was unperceived by the 77th, who rushed on, with the exception of about a dozen, who struck by the force on our left, and who saw me taking out my revolver, halted with me. "Come on," I said, "my lads!" and the brave fellows dashed in amongst the astonished Russians, bayoneting them in every direction. One of the bullets of my revolver had partly come out and prevented it revolving and I could not get it off. The Russians fired their pieces off within a few yards of my head, but none touched me. I drew my sword and cut off one man's arm who was in the act of bayoneting me and a second seeing it, turned round and was in the act of running out of my way, when I hit him over the back of the neck and laid him dead at my feet. About 15 of them threw down their arms and gave themselves up and the remainder ran back and fell into the hands of the 77th returning from the splendid charge they had made and were killed or taken prisoner.' Clifford was awarded the Victoria Cross. In May 1855, he was appointed deputy Assistant Quartermaster-General, which post he held until the end of the war, being promoted to the rank of brevet major.

Men of the 77th Regiment in winter clothing much as they might have looked at the battle. It was spring and early summer when Fenton was in the Crimea and the weather was warm. For photographs such as this one Fenton asked the men to dress up in their winter clothes for the camera.

Fenton described this photograph as that of a sergeant of light infantry. The man in question actually belongs to the 21st Fusiliers. It would appear that Fenton was confused by the man's shoulder 'wings' which were normally worn by light infantry companies. However the uniforms of the Fusilier regiments also carried such wings. At Inkerman, the 21st Fusiliers, along with the 88th and 77th regiments, helped drive the Russians off Shell Hill at the height of the battle.

A Horse Artillery team with gun carriage and nine-pounder gun. 'The Royal Artillery deserve the greatest credit for the part they played at the battle of Inkerman,' wrote Major Ewart of the 93rd Highlanders, 'as the Russian guns were much more numerous, and most of them of heavier calibre, than those of the British. Altogether there were thirty-six British field-guns (9-pounder guns and 24-pounder howitzers), besides the two 18-pounders; the French brought into action eighteen of their guns; so the allies had just fifty-six guns, opposed to ninety-four Russian ones – fifty-four of the latter being 12-pounder and 32-pounder howitzers.'

Two French officers posing for Fenton, along with a Zouave. The arrival of the French secured victory for the Allies at Inkerman. Altogether the French committed around 9,000 men and twenty-four artillery pieces to the battle and suffered 229 killed and 1,551 wounded.

Two Zouaves. Dressed, in Fenton's words, in 'garb of many colours' these highly regarded élite troops were originally raised in Algeria as light infantry battalions. When the Zouaves attacked at Inkerman, Jean Cler, a Colonel of the 2nd Zouaves told his men, 'Spread out your pants as wide as they will go, and make as big a show of yourselves as you can.' Sergeant Gowing, of the 7th Fusiliers, wrote: 'We hear that the Zouaves fought like so many tigers, and although the odds were heavily against them, they routed the enemy off the field. I don't think I ever told you before that they are not all Frenchmen that wear French uniforms. The Zouaves have a number of English and Irish mixed up with them – wild spirits that join them on account of rapid promotion.'

This second photograph of Zouaves, shows a wounded private being attended to by a fellow Zouave NCO and a cantinière. Fenton was particularly impressed with the Zouaves, as many of the British troops were, and he even had a photograph of himself taken wearing Zouave uniform. The above photo, however, is a *tableaux vivant*, in other words a posed scene.

Colonel Dickson. Though described by Fenton as being a member of the Royal Engineers, Lieutenant Colonel, later General Sir Collingwood Dickson served with the Royal Artillery and earlier, on 17 October 1854, when the batteries had run short of powder, Dickson 'displayed great coolness and contempt of danger in directing the unloading of several waggons of the field battery which were brought up to the trenches to supply the want. He personally helped to carry the powder-barrels under heavy fire from the enemy.' This action earned Dickson the Victoria Cross.

Shown here is the 57th Regiment, the charge of which along with the 55th and 77th was one of the final acts of the Battle of Inkerman. The course of the battle is regarded as being particularly difficult to follow and Fenton wrote that 'I have been there [Inkerman] now three times, and with people who were in the battle, and none can tell me where any of the principal incidents took place.' In his report on the battle Raglan himself wrote: 'The morning was extremely dark with a drizzling rain, rendering it almost impossible to discover anything beyond the flash and smoke of artillery and heavy musketry fire.'

Fenton gave this photograph the caption 'Lieutenant Colonel C.F. Seymour, Scots Fusilier Guards'. Seymour was General Cathcart's Assistant-Adjutant-General. He was shot through the body and then bayoneted whilst trying to help Cathcart after the General had been fatally wounded. In reporting Seymour's death, Lord Raglan wrote, 'he was remarkable for his intelligence, gallantry and zeal'. He was thirty-five years old. What does not make sense is that the Battle of Inkerman, and therefore Seymour's death, occurred before Fenton reached the Crimea.

Two views of the Cemetery on Cathcart's Hill. After his death Cathcart was buried on one of the hills close to the headquarters of the 4th Division, as has been known as Cathcart Hill ever since. The place became the site of a major British and French cemetery. In this photograph the soldier is standing before the grave of Brigadier-General Thomas Leigh Goldie who was also killed at the Battle of Inkerman whilst in command of Cathcart's 1st Brigade.

Chapter Seven

The Siege of Sevastopol

Siege operations continued throughout the winter. The Russians worked hard on Sevastopol's defences whilst the Allies sapped towards the city, moving the breaching batteries and the assaulting troops ever closer.

On the night of 22 February 1855, the hill of the Mamelon Vert was converted by the Russians into a redoubt faced with stone. It was opposite the French parallels and it was the French that attempted to capture the redoubt before its defences became too firmly established. They attacked and captured the Mamelon Vert but were unable to hold it. The battle for possession of the redoubt lasted for four days at the end of which the Mamelon Vert was still in Russian hands.

On 2 March Tsar Nicholas died but his son, Alexander II, had no intention of succumbing to the Allied nations especially as there was no sign of Sevastopol falling, the siege progressing slowly due to a lack of ammunition and with large numbers of men falling sick with cholera and typhus. 'We are all anxiously waiting for Lord Raglan to storm Sevastopol,' wrote Henry Clifford, 'for though we must lose many in doing it, yet anything would be better than seeing our fine soldiers dying as they are daily. What should be done is to go at once with no more dilly-dallying.'[26]

Finally, with fresh supplies of ammunition the Allies began the Second Bombardment of Sevastopol on 9 April. Together the Allies counted an impressive 500 guns (138 British and 362 French) but the defenders had amassed 998 pieces. The Allied armament, however, now included 13-inch naval mortars which could lob their shells into the heart of the city.

The bombardment severely damaged the Flagstaff Bastion and completely silenced the guns on the Mamelon. Raglan was for an assault immediately following the bombardment. Canrobert, though, could not support this as he had received instructions from Napoleon III ordering a wide distribution of his forces. Feeling that his authority had been compromised he resigned his command, which was passed on to General Pélissier.

The new French commander was not willing to delay an assault and on 7 June his men assaulted the Mamelon and the adjacent White Works, after a two-day bombardment. They stormed the Mamelon but were so inspired by their success they carried their attack onto the Malakoff Tower. The tower proved too great an obstacle and they were driven back by the Russians who then swept the attackers off the Mamelon.

The French rallied and again charged into the Mamelon. The recapture of the Mamelon was the signal for the British forces to attack the Russian positions in front of the Redan. Some 700 men of the Light and 2nd Divisions stormed the rifle pits, driving out the Russian sharpshooters.

The Allies were able to hold onto their gains, and the successes of 7 June paved the way for what was supposed to be the final great assault eleven days later. Throughout 17 June the Allied artillery pounded the city. The following morning the attack began.

The attackers, both French and British were met with a hail of canister and bullets. Both attacks failed with heavy casualties.

After the success of 7 June, hopes had been high. Now disappointment blanketed the Allied army and a severe outbreak of cholera added to the air of gloom and despair. 'I have not known any period during the siege when people so openly complain of their being heartily tired of it,' wrote Captain Maxwell Earle of the 57th Regiment. 'There is nothing going forward at present, and we can look forward to nothing. Before the attack of 18th of June when there was hope of terminating the siege I took an interest in watching the operations of the Enemy. Now whole days pass sometimes without my ever going 20 yards to look at the town.'[27]

As well as despondency, cholera swept through the British encampment and at the British headquarters, Sir James Estcourt, the Adjutant-General died followed, four days later, by Lord Raglan. Sir George Brown was the man nominated to replace Raglan in the event of just such an eventuality, but following the success of the Kertch expedition he had also been taken ill and he was already under medical orders to return to the UK. Command, therefore, fell upon Sir James Simpson.

On 16 August it was the Russians who attacked, and in considerable strength. With four infantry divisions, supported by artillery, they made a bid to capture the Fedioukine Heights. The attack failed and its failure marked the last Russian attempt at lifting the siege.

The following day the Allies opened their fifth bombardment of Sevastopol with 182 British and 522 French guns. The defences of Sevastopol mounted 1,209 artillery pieces of various calibres. The bombardment continued for a week. The assault was planned for 8 September, the artillery bombardment intensifying on the three preceding days. This final barrage is said to have been the heaviest in history up to that date.[28]

The main French objectives were the Malakoff and the Flagstaff Bastion. The British had the Redan. Amongst the leading ladder parties was that of the 97th Regiment and Major Welsford was the first man to force his way through the embrasures, followed by Captain Grove with the storming party of the 90th Regiment. A familiar story now followed. Under heavy fire the assaulting regiments became mixed, as Captain

Edmund Legh of the 97th explained: 'Men of other Regts. principally 90th, 3rd & 41st then came to help us; & the parties got so mixed and jammed together that one could not get a formation for a rush. Just at this time, the enemy driven out of the Malakoff, took us in flank, and by keeping up a heavy fire killed a great number of men. They profited by this, made a charge, and by their superior numbers drove our men into an angle of the Redan, where from behind 2 Guns, they kept up a vigorous fire for nearly 2 hours.'[29]

Both sides continued to fire at each other, and both sides began to run out of ammunition. When the Russians ran out of bullets they picked up stones and threw them at the attackers — some even threw their muskets at the British. Surprisingly, it was this hail of stones that finally decided the day. The attackers turned and ran in utter confusion.

The British assault upon the Redan had failed ignominiously but it mattered little, because their allies had succeeded. The French had taken and held the Malakoff. The tower was the key to Sevastopol's defences and in enemy hands it rendered the southern half of the city untenable.

During the night loud explosions were heard from within the city and the entire population of the place crossed the harbour on a pontoon bridge to the north side. After eleven months of proud defiance, the Russian had finally given up Sevastopol.

Roger Fenton left the Crimea in June 1855, being replaced by James Robertson and therefore did not witness the capture of Sevastopol. Fortunately Robertson did, and his photographs of Sevastopol are amongst the last images of the war in the Crimea but they were not the last images relating to the Crimean War, as we will see.

*   *   *

Though the southern, and principal, part of Sevastopol was in Allied hands, war wasn't quite over yet. The Russians consolidated their position on the North Side and the opposing artillery fired sporadically and ineffectually at each other across the water. On 11 November 1855, a disillusioned Sir James Simpson resigned his command and handed over the army to Sir William Codrington.

Peace moves, however, were afoot. With Austria acting as the broker a deal was put together which was accepted by both sides. The terms demanded by the Allies, and agreed to by Russia, included the neutralisation of the Black Sea — Britain's and France's war aims had been achieved.

On 29 February 1856, the guns fell silent and the formal end of the Crimean War came a month later with the signing of the Treaty of Paris on 30 March. As to which religious group should hold the keys to the holy places in Bethlehem — the subject was not even mentioned.

A succession of photographs in which Fenton attempted to show the British army's positions during the siege. This first one shows the encampments of tents and huts on the plateau of Cathcart's Hill, looking towards the Light Division with Inkerman in the distance. The one below shows the camp of the 4th Division with General Garrett's quarters in the centre. The third one is of the camp of the 3rd Division with the tents of the French corps just visible in the distance.

Captain, later General Sir Edward Stanton, KCB, KCMG, was commissioned as a Second Lieutenant in the Royal Engineers on 19 February 1827, and played an important part in the siege operations before Sevastopol. After the Crimean War he remained in the area, being part of the boundary commission that determined the Russo-Turkish borders. Stanton followed a political career becoming Consular-General firstly in Poland and later in Egypt.

Captain Holder of the Fusilier Guards. The Crimean War would become notable for the terrible conditions the troops had to endure, but this clearly did not extend to the privileged officers. When Fenton dined with Captain Holder, the meal consisted of 'gravy soup, fresh fish caught in the bay, liver and bacon fried, a shoulder of mutton, pancakes with quince preserve, cheese, stout, sherry and cigars'. The next morning Fenton was woken by Holder's servant with a cup of hot chocolate, and they then had a breakfast of potted tongue, tea, toast, fish and marmalade.

A general view (above) and a close-up (below) of the British Green Hill battery, known as the 'Left Attack'. This was under the direction of an Engineer officer, Captain Chapman. The left and right attacks were separated by the Worontzoff Ravine. This battery was attacked by the Russians on 21 December at 02:30 hours. Though only lasting for around thirty minutes, the result were quite significant as the Russians captured two officers and another thirty-six were either killed, wounded or missing. (*Courtesy of the King's Own Royal Regiment Museum*)

'Captain Walker reading orders.' Walker transferred from the 30th Regiment to the 3rd Regiment and he recorded in his journal what happened during the first attack upon the Redan: 'While I was in the act of hurrying the men up a howitzer shell dropped beside me and exploded. A piece struck me on the right elbow and smashed it. I immediately tied a large handkerchief above the fracture and walked to the rear.' Walker's arm was amputated.

Captain Maxwell Earle served as Major of Brigade under Brigadier-General Philip McPherson. McPherson is shown sitting here with Earle standing immediately to his right. In this group are other officers of the 4th Division, Captain Heigham and Captain Croker of the 17th Regiment as well as Captain Swire and Captain McPherson. Earle regarded McPherson as an 'old nonentity'. He said that if he was to put McPherson's own death warrant on his desk in front of him he would sign it! The 17th were involved in the attack of 18 June. 'It was an a[w]ful day it being the first General Action I was in,' wrote a private of the 17th. 'I can[n]ot Describe the sensations I felt Peculiar to young Soldiers on being formed up to front the enemy for the first time. When we were waiting behind the trench and got the order to fix Bayonets and cap our firelocks … I began to feel as if I would like to be at home.'

Captain J.L. Croker of the 17th Regiment. In the attack of 18 June the 17th Regiment were met with a hail of fire as soon as they had emerged from the network of trenches in front of the Redan. In the confined space they could achieve little by way of formation and their progress was impeded by the dead and wounded of previous attempts. Captain Croker was killed along with thirteen other ranks; a further thirty-two other ranks were wounded. Great bravery was shown by a number of men who went back to bring in the body of Captain Croker, and in particular by Corporal Philip Smith who several times brought in wounded men under fire. Smith was awarded the Victoria Cross.

Captain Wilkinson of the 9th Regiment. In the attack of 18 June, the 9th Regiment drove the Russians out of Sevastopol Cemetery and occupied some of the nearby houses but, with the failure of the attempt upon the Redan found itself under fire from the twenty-one gun 'Strand' Battery unable to either advance or retreat. The 9th held its ground from 04.00 hours to 21.00 hours. '17 hours under a tremendous fire of shot, shell, grape, canister, & hundreds of their sharpshooters,' wrote Wilkinson's fellow officer, Scott, 'our only cover being the houses which crumbled about us at every discharge.'

Lieutenant Colonel James Shadforth, shown here at his hut along with officers of the 57th Regiment. It was at the siege of Sevastopol that the actions of two members of the 57th Regiment resulted in the award of the Victoria Cross. On 22 March 1855, Sergeant (later Colour-Sergeant) Gardiner acted 'with great gallantry upon the occasion of a sortie by the enemy, in having rallied the covering parties which had been driven in by the Russians, thus regaining the trenches. On 18th June during the attack on the Redan he himself remained and encouraged others to remain in the holes made by the explosions of the shells, and from whence they were able to keep up a continuous fire until their ammunition was exhausted, and the enemy cleared away from the parapet.' The second member of the 57th Regiment to be awarded the Victoria Cross at Sevastopol was Private Charles McCorrie. On 23 June he picked up a live Russian shell and threw it over the parapet, thus saving the lives of the men around him. James Shadforth, who had only become a Lieutenant Colonel in November 1854, was killed in the attack of 18 June, shortly after leaving the trenches.

Officers from the 14th Regiment: Captain Barlow; Captain Trevor; Captain Hall; Captain Dwyer; Major Budd; and Captain Hammersley. The 14th Regiment was not involved at the battles of Alma or Inkerman but did take part in the first assault upon the Redan. Being the battalion's first major engagement the troops were anxious for the action to begin: 'The men, being excited, did not go to sleep but remained up till we were directed to fall in at midnight,' recalled the 14th's commanding officer, Lieutenant Colonel Sir James Alexander. 'Our camp looked like a fair. Lighted up, with a buzz of voices everywhere. The Russians must have remarked this.'

Lieutenant-Colonel Sir Frederick Edward Chapman CB, Royal Engineers. On the declaration of war Chapman was attached to the First Division, commanded by the Duke of Cambridge, as senior engineer officer, with Captain Montagu's company of royal sappers and miners under his orders. He took part in the Battle of the Alma, and was mentioned in despatches of 28 September 1854. In October he was appointed to the command, as director, of the left British attack at the Siege of Sevastopol, and continued in this post until 22 March 1855, when Major (afterwards Major General Sir) John William Gordon the director of the Right British attack, was severely wounded. Chapman became executive engineer for the whole siege operations under Sir Harry Jones.

Edward of Saxe-Weimar was born to Prince Bernhard of Saxe-Weimar-Eisenach and Princess Ida of Saxe-Meiningen. His military career began in 1841, when he joined the British 67th Regiment as an ensign. He became a major in the Grenadier Guards on 20 June 1854. He was promoted to the brevet rank of lieutenant colonel 'for distinguished Service in the Field' including the siege. Fenton described him as 'a very nice quiet fellow, plain but a good figure, and seems a favourite here.' He was particularly affected by the scenes after the Battle of Inkerman, writing: 'Never shall I forget the sight of the dead and dying Russians on the field. Some of the poor wretches had to lie on the field for at least sixty hours before they were removed to the hospital tents; the majority of course died.' He eventually became a Field Marshal.

Brigadier Garrett with officers of the 46th Regiment. When the 46th arrived to reinforce the army in the Crimea, in November 1854, Captain William Radcliffe was amazed at how they looked: 'such a contrast to the men that have been here for some time; they look as clean as new pins, & are easily recognised by their white belts & blankets.' The arrival of reinforcements was much welcomed and, according to Temple Godman, they were 'greatly cheered by the French who brought their bands out to play them by.'

Robertson's photograph of the French trenches and their zigzag saps running up to the Malakoff on the hill in the distance. In the foreground is a howitzer battery.

Henry J. Brownrigg, Deputy Assistant Commissary General, was attached to the 3rd Division since their landing in the Crimea. During that time he was in charge of the commissariat of the division's 2nd Brigade. During the month of January 1855, Brownrigg was in temporary charge of the commissariat of both brigades of the division.

(*Facing page*) In December 1854 a large number of reinforcements reached the Crimea including the 89th Regiment, a group of officers of which are shown here. They are, from left to right: Captain Hawley; Captain Skynner; Major Egerton; Major Watson; Major Aylmer; and Captain Cuppage. Raglan complained about the calibre of the reinforcements: 'I wish that we had older men than those sent out. Some of the drafts lately come out are little more than sixteen years of age and there is a boy with my guard who only enlisted nine weeks ago, and tho' professing to be sixteen looks I am told about fourteen.'

Captain Lilley of the Field Train. Transportation was a considerable problem during the siege and this led to the formation of the Land Transport Corps in 1855. After the war the Land Transport Corps was re-organized as the Military Train.

Fenton described this photograph as 'A quiet day in the mortar battery'. The mortars were fired at a fixed elevation of forty-five degrees. Once the range was found, they could be fired repeatedly without being re-laid. For this reason they were mainly kept for use at night, which is why Fenton thought that it was a quiet day, in reality, it was most probably just a normal day.

'Mortar batteries in front of Picquet house, Light Division.' Fenton went to the mortar battery on 29 April 1855, which was normally forbidden to everyone except for staff officers and people on duty. The British had three types of mortars in the Crimea, the largest of which threw a thirteen-inch shell 2,700 yards.

Arthur John Layard was a Captain in the 38th Regiment. He was aide-de-camp to Lieutenant General Pennefather. Layard had a poor opinion of Lord Raglan, writing that he 'cannot make up his mind to do anything and is undecided in everything'. Layard repeatedly complained about the management of the army and it soon became suspected at Raglan's HQ that Layard was the author of letters published in *The Times* which were severely critical of Raglan and the heads of the various departments. He died of cholera, aged thirty-six, in August 1855.

The Reverend H.P. Wright, principal chaplain to the forces in the Crimea, and Reverend Messieurs Wallace, Sykes, Parson, H.A. Taylor, Boudier, Parker, Preston and Crozier. Henry Press Wright was the only chaplain to sail with the British army in 1854. However, the reports of William Russell in *The Times* caused the Society for the Propagation of the Gospel to finance more chaplains. Eventually sixty were sent to the Crimea, of who twelve died. After the fall of Sevastopol, Reverend Wright had to preside over a mass funeral service for more than 700 men. 'The newly turned earth in the half-filled trench was their only grave,' wrote Fanny Duberly, 'and the frowning battery their grand and solemn monument'.

Brigadier-General Charles Thomas (later General Sir) Van Straubenzee, shown seated in the middle of a group of officers of the 3rd Regiment. Van Straubenzee sailed with the 'Buffs' for the Crimea on 14 April 1855 and joined Sir Colin Campbell's Highland Division, taking command of what was called the 'Separate Brigade' consisting of the 3rd, 31st and 72nd regiments. He led his brigade at the fight at the Quarries on 7 June. On 30 July he was appointed to command the 1st Brigade of the Light Division and took part in both assaults on the Redan. He was wounded in the attack of 8 September and was Mentioned in Despatches in *The London Gazette* on 3 October 1855.

The French Colonel Vico was attached to the British Headquarters. Raglan made particular mention of him in his despatch on the Battle of the Alma, writing that he 'afforded me all the assistance in his power, sparing no exertion to be of use'. Vico died of cholera on 12 July 1855. Despite the efforts of the Sanitary Committee, the conditions remained very poor long after they had begun their work. Around 90,000 French soldiers died in the Crimea of which around 60,000 died of disease, mainly typhus and cholera.

Throughout the siege the Russians had been receiving supplies of food, guns and ammunition from the north through the port of Kertch (or Kerch) which controlled the supply lines across the Sea of Azov. Raglan was instructed to cut off this supply. After an abortive effort in the first week of May 1855, a force of some 15,000 French, Turkish and British troops set off on 24 May on sixty ships of the Allied fleet, the whole being under the command of Sir George Brown. The British contingent included the 71st Regiment, a group of which are shown here.

A photograph of ships of the French Navy taken in the Sea of Azov during the Kertch campaign. The French ships were under the command of Admiral Bruat, those of the Royal Navy were under Sir Edmund Lyons. The campaign opened with a brief bombardment from the ships but there was no reply from the shore. Under the fleet's guns Brown's men landed unopposed at Ambalaki, a few miles south of Kertch. 'The French landed first in beautiful style,' remembered Fenton who went along on the expedition, 'then our men, marching away as they landed to get on to the ridge of the high land above the flat beach.' Shortly afterwards explosions could be heard as the Russians destroyed their own batteries and barracks, and the Russians abandoned Kertch without offering any resistance.

George William Hamilton FitzMaurice, 6th Earl of Orkney joined the 71st Highland Regiment as a Captain from the 92nd Regiment in 1853 and took part in the Kertch expedition with the regiment. Fenton watched the highlanders enter the town: 'Not a soul of the inhabitants were to be seen; all had left, we saw some of the last with our glasses in the morning from the ships, going away in carts, and one group left the village while the French were firing shells into it to protect the disembarkation. While we were packing up the French had marched up in the van followed by the Turks, and the 79th, 42nd, 93rd, and 71st Highland regiments brought up the rear ... a beautiful sight it was to see them marching down the reverse of the hills on which we stood. There were no Russians in sight.' George FitzMaurice transferred to the Scots Fusilier Guards in 1856 and retired from the Army in 1857.

Captain Graham and Captain Macleod of the 42nd Regiment. The 42nd (Black Watch) Regiment also took part in the expedition to Kertch. The expedition was a great success. A hundred guns were captured, thousands of tons of corn and flour were destroyed, arsenals, factories and magazines were blown up and Russian ships sunk. The troops added to the destruction in an orgy of looting. Hardly a house was left untouched and everything that could be moved was taken away. What could not be moved was burnt or smashed. A French garrison was left in Kertch whilst the Allied warships sailed into the Sea of Azov seizing or destroying everything that could be found. 'It was like bursting into a vast treasure house crammed with wealth of inestimable value,' wrote one observer. 'For miles along its shores stretched the countless storehouses packed with the accumulated harvests of the great corn provinces of Russia. From them the Russian armies in the field were fed; from them the beleaguered population of Sevastopol looked for preservation from the famine which already pressed hard upon them.'

In the attack of 18 June on the Redan the 38th Regiment suffered very heavy casualties. The following day Fenton took this picture which shows what he called 'the remains' of the 38th's Light Company. They are being inspected here by Lieutenant General Sir John Campbell.

This is one of Robertson's photographs of one of the British siege batteries. When Fenton visited earlier in 1855, he wrote that: 'In the battery I was very comfortable, for the wall sheltered me, only it struck me as a queer sensation to hear the balls thumping into the earth against which one was leaning. Others came topping the ramparts and whistling overhead.' (*Courtesy of the King's Own Royal Regiment Museum*)

On 16 August 1855, the Russians attacked the Allied positions yet again. To reach the Allied siege lines the Russians had to cross the River Tchernaya. This is a photograph of the river and the Traktirny (or Tactir) bridge. The Allies were expecting an attack and the French and Sardinians were waiting. The attack was a disaster, with the Russians being driven back over the bridge, losing some 8,000 men. 'I rode over the ground just after,' remembered Temple Godman. 'It is a terrible sight when the excitement is over to see men torn in messes by round shot and shell, and then the wounded moaning and dying all around. If king's ministers could see a few such sights I think countries would not be hurried into war.' It was the last Russian offensive of the war.

Captain Pechell of the 77th. On 3 September 1855 Captains William Parker and Pechell were posting sentries in front of the siege works when they were attacked by a party of Russians. All the men were killed, including Pechell, except for Parker and one other man. Parker sent that man back to report the Russian attack whilst he tried to hold them at bay. He shot two of them with his revolver and eventually succeeded in taking Pechell's body back to camp. A statue of Pechell charging the enemy can be seen in the grounds of Stanmer Park, Brighton. William Parker was killed five days later and he also has a memorial, this one, though, is in Halifax, Nova Scotia.

An officer and NCO of the 57th Regiment. 'I have not known any period during the siege when people so openly complain of their being heartily tired of it,' wrote Captain Maxwell Earle of the 57th. 'There is nothing going forward at present, and we can look forward to nothing. Before the attack of 18th of June when there was hope of terminating the siege I took an interest in watching the operations of the Enemy. Now whole days pass sometimes without my ever going 20 yards to look at the town.'

Officers of the 89th Regiment at Cathcart's Hill, in winter dress for the sake of the camera. They are Captain Skynner, Lieutenant Knatchbull, Captain Conyers, Lieutenant Longfield and Captain Hawley. Captain Robert Hawley was highly critical of Codrington's direction of the assault upon the Redan and when he learnt that Codrington was to take over command of the army from Simpson, he wrote: 'The appointment of Codrington surely is unwise. It does not please the Army, for with it on the 8th he lost caste entirely.'

Men of the 3rd Regiment piling arms. Two members of the 3rd Regiment were awarded the Victoria Cross for actions during the siege. During the assault upon the Redan on 8 September, Private John Connors went to the help of an officer of the 30th Regiment in the Redan who was surrounded by Russians. In command of the 3rd was Brevet Lieutenant Colonel (later General) Frederick Maude. During the attack of the 8th, he was responsible for the covering party and the ladder party of the 2nd Division. He held a traverse with only nine or ten men until all hope of support was lost, despite being severely wounded. This is another of Fenton's staged photographs showing the various uniforms worn. The individual on the left of the photo is wearing the 'Kilmarnoc' cap and greatcoat, whilst those piling arms are wearing the 'Albert' shakos and red coatees.

Officers of the 90th Regiment. Captain Robert Grove was with the storming party of the 90th Regiment and he described the confusion of the assault: 'The eager trying to pass others more orderly, and as the ladders could not accommodate all, a mixture of corps took place, scrambling became the order of the day and as we could offer no front to our enemy (having no frontage of ladders) we fell an easy prey to the concentrated fires of the Russians.'

Brigadier General Henry Frederick Lockyer and two of his staff of the 97th Regiment. Lockyer, of Brompton Kent, survived the Crimean War and rose to the rank of Major General. He became commander-in-chief of British forces in Ceylon and died at sea on 30 August 1860.

Officers of the 88th Regiment. Captain Nathaniel Steevens of the 88th witnessed the retreat from the Redan: 'The dense mass of humanity which thronged the Redan was carried headlong into the Ditch, upon the top of bayonets, ladders and dead & dying, writhing in their agony under the crush of us all; I found myself jammed under a scaling ladder, firelocks between my legs, and the Russians pelting stones from the parapet 6 or 8yds from me.' Nathaniel Steevens was commissioned ensign in the 20th (The East Devonshire) Regiment of Foot on 19 December 1845, transferring to the 88th Regiment of Foot (Connaught Rangers) in 1850. Promoted captain on 27 October 1854, he served throughout the Crimean campaign.

'I went to the Redan,' wrote Captain Temple Godman. 'The Russians were there in heaps, and the ditch was nearly full of dead English piled one on the other, I suppose five feet thick or more. The Redan was terribly strong, and bombproof inside. There was not a place an inch large that was not ploughed up by our shot and shell, guns, gabions; and even pieces of human flesh of every shape and size were scattered about, it was absolutely torn to pieces, and one mass of rubbish and confusion impossible to describe.'

(*Facing page*) Following the storming of Sevastopol, Robertson was able to photograph inside the Russian defensive works. The above is a view of the Barracks Battery and below is a photograph of the interior of the Redan. Fanny Duberly described the nature of the Russian works: 'The Redan is a succession of little batteries, each containing two or three guns, with traverses behind each division; and hidden away under gabions, sand-bags, and earth, are little huts in which the officers and men used to live ... The centre, the open space between the Redan and the second line of defence, was completely ploughed by our thirteen-inch shells, fragments of which, together with round shot, quite paved the ground.'

The interior of the Malakoff tower after its capture by the French. Once again it was the Zouaves who performed with great vigour in the capture of the Malakoff. In the attack of 8 September, they poured out of their sap and ran the twenty-five yards to the Malakoff, siezing it from the startled Russians. They then raised the Tricolour over the Malakoff fort which was the signal for the British assault upon the Redan.

(*Facing page*) This is one of the photographs taken by Colonel Jean-Charles Langlois shortly after the capture of the Malakoff. The title which this has been given is simply 'sturdy cannon and fortifications, Crimea'. Temple Godman visited the Malakoff at this time, which he described as an 'extraordinary' sight. 'The French lay in piles, where they had been mown down by the grape from a steamer, and the Russians too were in lines where the French had brought up field-pieces, and sent grape among masses at a few yards. I could form no idea of the number dead, which must be enormous – it beats anything I have ever seen before.'

The Russian generals' bomb-proof shelter in the Redan after the dead had been taken away. Captain Scott of the 9th Regiment had the task of burying the dead that lay in the Redan: 'We put about 250 English and 150 Russians into the ditch at the angle of the Redan, and filled it on them from both sides. Besides those we buried several detached parties of Ruskies in different holes about the work. *Never* had to perform such a disgusting duty. The bodies were so mangled, and some of the Ruskies had been dead for days.'

The plenipotentiaries at the signing of the Peace of Paris in 1856. Standing, from left to right: Baron von Hübner (Austria); Ali Pasha (Turkey); Earl of Clarendon (British Foreign Secretary); Count Walewski (France); Count Orloff (Russia); Baron de Bourqueney (France); Earl Cowley (British Ambassador). Seated, left to right: Count Cavour (Sardinia); de Villamarina (Sardinia); Graf von Hatzfeldt (Prussia); Baron von Manteuffel (Prussia); and Graf von Buol (Austria).

(*Facing page*) Mary Jane Seacole was well educated and skilled Jamaican nurse and when the Crimean War broke out she travelled to London and applied to go to the Crimea to tend to the wounded soldiers. However because of her race she was not granted an interview by the British War Office. She then applied to Elizabeth Herbert, the wife of the Secretary of State for War who was recruiting nurses for the war effort but was again denied an interview. Seacole then went on her own initiative and in 1856 established the British Hotel near Balaklava at her own expense. She provided comfortable quarters for the sick and convalescent and often went to the battlefield to attend to the wounded. After the war Mary Seacole was bankrupt but her story was carried by the British press and money was raised to pay off her debts.

Chapter Eight

Aftermath

News of the Treaty of Paris reached the Crimea on 1 April 1856. The next day the Allied guns in the Crimea fired for the last time, in a salute to mark the end of the war. Under the terms of the treaty the Allies were given six months to evacuate the Crimea, which would involve a huge logistical effort, to compile and transport in a few months the enormous amount of *materiel* which had been accumulated over the course of two years. Much had simply to be abandoned, and most of the horses and mules were sold off to the local Russian population.

As well as selling off the animals, the railway was sold to a company that proposed building a new railroad between Jaffa and Jerusalem. The project failed to materialise and in the end the Balaklava line was sold to the Turks as scrap.

On 12 July, Codrington formally handed back possession of Balaklava to a Russian delegation and sailed away with the last British troops on HMS *Algeria*. He left behind the remains of 20,813 men who had died during the war, 20 per cent of all those that served in the Crimea. The total deaths in the conflict amounted to around 650,000, the vast majority being from the Russian Army.

The Crimean War had been the most destructive of Queen Victoria's reign and throughout the conflict she had been anxious to hear about the welfare of the soldiers. Copies of some of the soldiers' letters were circulated for her information; some she would later acquire for her own collection. One such document, a copy of a letter sent by Captain Gordon, Scots Fusilier Guards, from a camp near Sevastopol on 6 December 1854, included the following:

'We have had miserable work lately, perpetual rain for a fortnight which at times comes down by bucket-fulls. The men are very badly off, their clothes being completely worn out, our clothing which was due last May never having arrived and we are afraid it went to the bottom in 'The Prince' during the late gales, so the consequence is they are almost in a state of nudity, and many of them are obliged to wear white trousers as their blacks are worn out. There is some warm clothing at Balaklava, but owing to the Commissariat being so badly off for transport to bring it up, we cannot get it, the roads also are in a dreadful state ...

'We have got over 100 men sick in our Hospital tents and I am sorry to say that the cholera has broken out amongst us again, which is very sad as the sick have nothing to lie upon but the wet ground, our clergyman who has only just come out to us, visited our Hospitals up here for the first time yesterday, and told me "he expected to see them in a very bad state, but certainly he never thought they were as bad as they are."'[31]

In 1855, when the first batch of wounded men returned from the Crimea, Queen Victoria invited a small group of them to Buckingham Palace. The sight of these 'mutilated' men so affected her that the speech of welcome she had prepared 'all stuck in my throat' and she had to excuse herself from it for fear of breaking down.[32]

Despite this moving experience, the Queen would not be deterred. On a later occasion, as she watched some of the boatloads of men returning to Woolwich, Victoria was presented with a far different picture. She remarked that the returning troops were 'the picture of real fighting men, such fine tall strong men, some strikingly handsome – all with such proud, noble, soldier-like bearing … They all had long beards, and were heavily laden with large knapsacks, their cloaks and blankets on top, canteens and full haversacks, and carrying their muskets.'[33]

Queen Victoria and Prince Albert, accompanied by their two eldest sons, the Prince of Wales (later Edward VII) and Prince Alfred (later Duke of Edinburgh), met some of the wounded men who had returned from the Crimea at Chatham on 3 March 1855. This was the first of many visits made to Kent. In one ward, the Queen stopped to converse with Sergeant Leny, who had fought at the battles of the Alma, Balaklava, and Inkerman. Lying in bed next to him was the badly injured James Higgins, whose 'appearance caused much painful emotion to her Majesty'.

After visiting the military hospital at Fort Pitt, the Royal Party continued on to Brompton Barracks. It was there that Queen Victoria was introduced to a number of men whom she later sketched, almost certainly from memory. She described in her journal how Sergeant Scarff of the 17th Lancers 'told us how he had received his sabre cuts, one on his head, and one on his two hands, which he had put up to save his head'.

George Russell Dartnell, an army surgeon who was, at that time, Deputy Inspector-General of Hospitals, later recalled this royal visit: 'The patients here also were all brought down to the lower ward, every one of which Her Majesty visited, expressing the greatest sympathy for the wounded, enquiring into all their cases, greatly interested in the histories of their several exploits, but distressed apparently beyond measure at the vast number of maimed and disabled men.

'In one of the wards she took much notice of a fine looking young soldier, who was far advanced in Phthisis [pulmonary tuberculosis or a similar progressive systemic disease]. After leaving the ward, she sent Colonel Phipps back to tell the man that, if he wished, she would get him into the Consumption Hospital in London. Colonel Phipps on his return said, "The young man desires me to say that he is extremely grateful for your Majesty's kindness, but that he would prefer remaining where he is, as he is as comfortable as he could be anywhere".[34]

For over three hours, the Queen made her way from patient to patient. As for the convalescents, they were arranged in different rooms in the Officers' Mess House according to the battles in which they had been wounded, and on each door was fixed a card with the words 'Alma', 'Balaklava', or 'Inkerman' printed in large letters.

Before stepping into her carriage to depart, the Queen turned to Dartnell. 'Mr Dartnell,' she said, 'I wish you to send me time to time the names of any badly maimed men of good character who, you think, would derive comfort from the use of artificial limbs or other mechanical appliances of a more complete or expensive nature than those furnished by the Government.'[35]

Her Majesty's second visit to Chatham was made in June 1855; her third on 28 November the same year. On 16 April 1856, Queen Victoria undertook a fourth tour of Brompton Barracks to see convalescent soldiers recovering from their wounds. To greet her, a crowd of several hundred men was assembled.

The photographs of Fenton and Robertson also inspired Queen Victoria to commission her own collection of images. At her instruction, the photographers Joseph Cundall and Robert Howlett produced a series of commemorative portraits of soldiers and sailors, including many wounded, on their return.

Cundall was a Norfolk-born publisher and photographer and one of the founding members of what would become the Royal Photographic Society. Howlett, meanwhile, worked at the naval dockyards and the veteran's hospital at Woolwich. Operating chiefly in the summer of 1856, the pair set up a temporary studio in Aldershot as well as visiting various naval dockyards, military hospitals and barracks.

The Queen gave specific instructions to Cundall and Howlett as to how the men were to be photographed. Regimental group photographs, for example, were to show three or four of 'the most distinguished and handsome men', and were to be taken as soon as possible, as the Queen was afraid that they would shave or otherwise change their war-like appearance.

It was not only groups who were pictured. During a visit to Fort Pitt, Cundall and Howlett photographed Private Clemence Brophy of the 34th Foot. The atmospheric image that resulted shows Brophy leaning against a wall holding his pipe in his right hand.

Another amputee photographed at about the same time, though at Brompton Barracks, was Sergeant John Breese of the 11th (Prince Albert's Own) Hussars. Breese had lost his right arm at the Battle of Inkerman. He was one of the wounded men introduced to Queen Victoria and Prince Albert during one their tours of Brompton Barracks. Indeed, his picture was taken at the direct bidding of the Queen; he was later sketched by the monarch. Victoria was so moved by Breese's story, that she later appointed him a Yeoman of the Guard, with a pension for life (Breese died in 1889).

It was not just the wounded who were selected to be the subject of Cundall's and Howlett's work. Queen Victoria and Prince Albert had visited Woolwich Barracks on 13 March 1856, to witness the arrival of a party from the Royal Artillery returning from the Crimea. Two of those present were Trumpeter George Gritten, 11th Battalion, and Bugler William Lang, 12th Battalion. Again at the Queen's request, the pair was pictured posing with war trophies, including a trumpet, a Russian eagle flagstaff and a Russian gun (possibly one of those captured at Sevastopol). Aged twelve, Lang was thought to be the youngest soldier in the British Army at the time.

Some of those photographed might have been known to Queen Victoria. William Herbert J. Disbrowe entered the Army in 1854 and became a Lieutenant that same year. He served with the 17th Regiment of Foot and took part in the Siege of Sevastopol and the assault on Redan. Disbrowe returned to the United Kingdom after the war and remained with the regiment, though he is mentioned in the Army List of 1859–60 as having died but it does not say whether this was in action. The Disbrowe family would have been known to Queen Victoria, since several of its members had served in the Royal Household.

Sergeant Major Edward Edwards, Scots Fusilier Guards, who was the subject of a three-quarters length portrait, was well known to the Royal Family. Edwards had acted as Drilling Sergeant to the Prince of Wales and Prince Alfred since 1852. According to military records, Edwards never missed a day of duty during the entire Crimean Campaign. He received the Distinguished Conduct Medal with £20, the French *Médaille Militaire*, and, having fought at Alma, Balaklava, Inkerman and Sevastopol, the Campaign Medal with four clasps. Edwards was discharged in May 1860 in London, having previously participated in the triumphant march of the Guards Regiments to Buckingham Palace on 9 July 1856, a parade that was watched by the Queen and Royal Family.[35] Flowers were thrown at the men and the soldiers attached them to their fixed bayonets. In her journal, Queen Victoria noted: 'Sergeant Edwards marched proudly at the head of the Regt., carrying a bouquet of roses.' He went on to become Drilling Sergeant to the younger royal children.

The collection of photographs taken by Cundall and Howlett were eventually brought together in an album with the title Crimean Heroes and Trophies. They were also displayed at an exhibition.

Moved by the suffering and the bravery of the troops, the Queen, along with the Government, commissioned a Guards Memorial to commemorate the heroes of the war. On 26 June 1857, the Queen and Prince Albert attended a parade of Crimean veterans in Hyde Park. There, sixty-two veterans were chosen to receive the first of the small bronze medals in recognition of their outstanding valour – the Victoria Cross.

Having spent two years attempting to capture Sevastopol, the Allies had no intention of allowing the harbour to be used by the Russian fleet again for a long time and consequently set about destroying the docks. On 20 October 1855, Colonel Stephenson of the Scots Guards, echoed those sentiments: 'I took a most interesting walk yesterday over the Mamelon, the Malakoff, and the Karalbelnaya suburb including the celebrated docks, which are extremely fine work. It is, however, being mined in all directions, and the mines will not be completed for another month, although the sappers are working at them every day. I should think that at the end of that time they will explode them. It seems rather barbarous at first sight to destroy such beautiful works, which must have cost millions to construct, but considering that they formed part of a gigantic plan for conquest, and never can be used for any legitimate purpose, it would be folly to leave them untouched.'

The demolition of the docks began in December 1855, and was observed by an American journalist: 'Of the five celebrated dry docks in the Karabelnaia suburb, as represented above, one was demolished in December Last. Not in a month, or a week, or a day; but in one blast the massive fabric was almost instantaneously reduced to a heap of stones ... The report accompanying such a Titanian work of destruction, imagination would suggest to be like that which accompanies some awful convulsion of nature. But what was the case? It was heard in camp, but was generally supposed to be the bursting of some of the Russian projectiles among the buildings of the town. Nearer to the scene of the explosion, a tremulous agitation of the ground was felt; and this was followed by that peculiarly compressed sound — more like the rumbling of distant thunder, than the usual report of gunpowder fired from within metal — which always accompanies subterraneous discharges. Simultaneous with the noise of the blasting, the sky over the situation of the docks becomes clouded with smoke, stones and rubbish — masses of considerable size rise perpendicularly upwards — at the same time a shower of masonry is hurled from each side into the air, and curves towards the centre — a dense cloud of smoke rests over the place of ruin — a sort of terrific stillness pervades the atmosphere, and all is over.'

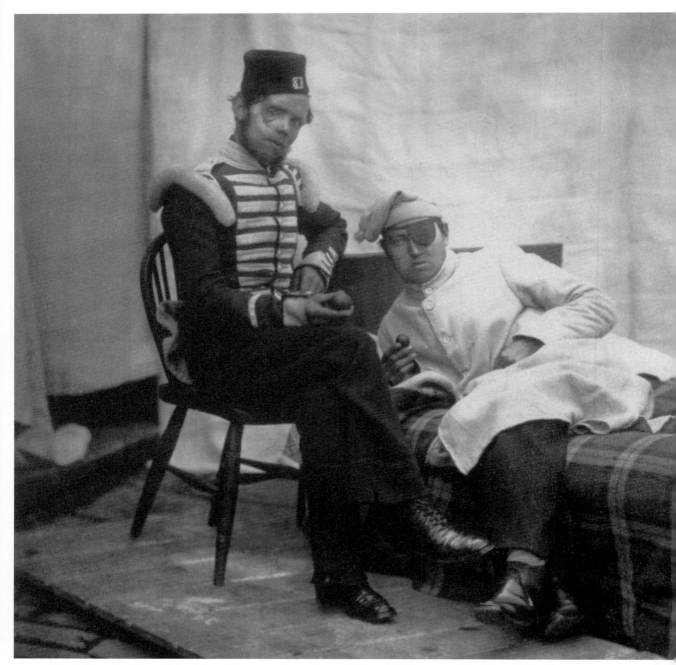

During her fourth and last visit to Brompton Barracks on 16 April 1856, several hundred soldiers were assembled to meet Queen Victoria. The Deputy Inspector-General of Hospitals, George Russell Dartnell, accompanied Her Majesty on her tour. He later wrote the following account: 'The inspection of this time occupied Her Majesty about three quarters of an hour. Many of the cases deeply attracted her attention and sympathy, especially those of two men who had been very severely wounded by grape shot in the face and head; two of these iron balls weighed 20ozs, each, another 13ozs. Photographic portraits were taken of these men.' The two wounded soldiers whose stories so moved the Queen, and who are seen here, were Private Jesse Lockhurst of the 31st Regiment, seated on the left, and Thomas O'Brien, 1st Royals. During fighting in 'advanced trenches' on 16 August 1855, Lockhurst received a shot in his right eye which destroyed its sight, as well as his upper jawbone. O'Brien had his left eye destroyed and his jawbone fractured at the Redan, 8 September 1855. In the photograph the Queen commissioned both men can be seen holding the shot which caused their injuries and which they had given to the Queen to hold in her own hand. (Royal Collection Trust/© Her Majesty Queen Elizabeth II)

The portrait of Private Clemence Brophy, of the 34th Foot, seated with his pipe leaning against a wall at Fort Pitt Military Hospital, Chatham, Kent. Born in Kilkenny, Ireland, Brophy joined the British Army, aged 21, on 21 December 1847. He lost his arm while fighting at Sevastopol on 31 August 1855. As a consequence of his injuries, Private Brophy was discharged from military service on 29 May 1856.

This photograph of a group of wounded soldiers, almost all of whom were from the Crimea, was taken at Brompton Barracks, Chatham during Queen Victoria's and Prince Albert's visit on 3 March 1855. The original caption provides information on some of the men. (*Royal Collection Trust/© Her Majesty Queen Elizabeth II*)

1	Corporal	David Williams	23rd Foot	Grape shot wound, left arm, Alma.
2	Private	James Alexander	30th Foot	Gunshot wound, left leg, Inkerman.
3	Private	James Doolan	19th Foot	Impaired health, Crimea.
4	Private	James Higgins	7th Foot	Amputation left leg after Alma.
5	Private	George Cope	93rd Foot	Gunshot wound, right leg, Sevastopol.
6	Private	Henry Pye	7th Foot	Cannon shot wound of both legs, Alma.
7	Private	John Smith	21st Foot	Gunshot wound, left leg, Inkerman.
8	Private	John O'Shaughnessy	41st Foot	Gunshot wound, right arm, Inkerman.
9	Private	William Frierillier	8th Foot	Impaired health, Crimea.
10	Private	Thomas Drew	93rd Foot	Wound, right leg, by a fall, Crimea.
11	Private	Henry Curther	37th Foot	Frostbite, right foot and both hands, trenches.
12	Corporal	Patrick O'Callaghan	30th Foot	Injuries of side by a fall, Crimea.
13	Private	Alfred Gibbs	Rifle Brigade	Frostbite, both feet, trenches.
14	Private	James Carkla	88th Foot	Frostbite, right foot, trenches.

15	Private	James Guest	7th Foot	Frostbite, right foot, trenches.
16	Private	Francis Ormond	20th Foot	Impaired health, Crimea.
17	Private	Charles Cardwell	47th Foot	Impaired health, Crimea.
18	Private	John Storey	Rifle Brigade	Impaired health, Crimea.
19	Private	Henry Minchen	Unknown	Impaired health, India.
20	Private	Benjamin Hall	4th Foot	Impaired health, Crimea.
21	Private	Mark Prires	97th Foot	Impaired health, Crimea.
22	Private	Robert Smith	34th Foot	Impaired health, Crimea.
23	Private	Edmund Glendon	14th Foot	Impaired health, Malta.
24	Private	Patrick McCarthy	34th Foot	Impaired health, Crimea.
25	Private	Daniel Grey	6 Dragoon Guards	Impaired health, Crimea.

Cundall's and Howlett's portrait of Colour Sergeant Absolom Durrant, Coldstream Guards, was probably taken during the preparations for the parade in London on 9 July 1856.

(*Facing page*) As the men gathered at Aldershot for the parade that was held in London on 9 July 1856, a number of them were photographed by Cundall and Howlett. This group shot of men of the 42nd (The Royal Highland) Regiment of Foot was one of those taken at the time. From left to right are: Piper David Muir, Piper George Glen, Piper Donald McKenzie and Colour Sergeant William Gardiner. All four are in uniform, though Glen's busby is on the floor under the table. Muir was 26-years-old when he was posted to the Crimea. He subsequently took part in an amphibious assault on Kertch whilst on an expedition. He also served at Balaklava, Sevastopol and Alma. Wounded at Alma, he received the Alma Medal and a Campaign Medal with three clasps. In October 2004, Muir was one of six men who were selected to appear on a series of commemorative stamps issued by the Royal Mail – his portrait formed the basis of the 1st class stamp. The other stamps featured Private Michael McNamara (2nd class), Sergeant Major Edward Edwards (40p), Sergeant William Powell (57p), Sergeant Major John Poole (68p), and Sergeant Robert Glasgow (£1.12p). Born in 1822, Private McNamara served in the 5th Dragoon Guards during the Crimean War. He took part in the Heavy Brigade charge at the Battle of Balaklava and fought at Inkerman and Sevastopol. Awarded a Campaign Medal with three clasps and £5 gratuity for Distinguished Conduct in Field, he was discharged from the army in 1867 as a Corporal. Sergeant Powell participated in the battles at Alma and Inkerman whilst in the ranks of the 3rd Battalion, the 1st (or Grenadier) Regiment of Foot Guards. A year after returning from the Crimea, he was discharged due to a reduction in the army. Sergeant Major Poole, on the other hand, served in the army for thirty years, all of which was in the Royal Sappers and Miners. During the Crimean War he participated in the Siege of Sevastopol as Sergeant Major of the Corps, and on the front lines on Inkerman Heights. He was awarded £10 annuity for long and meritorious conduct, and a Campaign Medal with one clasp. Featuring on the high denomination stamp, Sergeant Glasgow had originally enlisted in 1845. During the Crimean Campaign he had a very rapid rise through the ranks from Bombardier to Sergeant. He was awarded the Distinguished Conduct Medal when he was a Bombardier, and the Campaign Medal with four clasps (three from Crimea and one from India with the 14th Battalion of the Royal Artillery).

Notes

1. C.L. Bazancourt, Baron de, *Cinq mois devant Sébastopol. L'Expédition de Crimée jusqu' à la pris de Sébastopol* (Paris, 1855), quoted in R.L.V. ffrench Blake, *The Crimean War* (Pen & Sword, Barnsley, 2006), p. 47.
2. Timothy Gowing, *A Soldier's Experience, or, A Voice from the Ranks* (Thos Forman & Sons, Nottingham, 1903), p. 47.
3. Quoted in Ian Fletcher & Natalia Ishcenko, *The Battle of the Alma 1854, First Blood to the Allies in the Crimea* (Pen & Sword, Barnsley, 2008), p. 137.
4. Gowing, *op. cit.*, pp. 47–8.
5. Blake, *op. cit.*, pp. 56–7.
6. John Alexander Ewart, *The Story of a Soldier's Life, or, Peace, War, and Mutiny* (Sampson Low & Co., London, 1881), vol. I, pp. 230–1.
7. Quoted in Patrick Mercer, *'Give Them a Volley and Charge!' The Battle of Inkermann, 1854* (Spellmount, Stroud, undated), p. 25.
8. Though he was terminally ill with cancer, he actually died of a heart attack on the way to Constantinople, Orlando Figes, *Crimea: The Last Crusade* (Penguin, London, 2010), p. 229.
9. Alastair Massie, *The National Army Museum Book of the Crimean War: The Untold Stories* (Sidgwick & Jackson, London, 2004), pp. 62–3.
10. Blake, *op. cit.*, p. 71.
11. Alastair Massie, *op. cit.*, p. 79.
12. Christine Kelly, *Mrs Duberley's War: Journal & Letters From the Crimea* (Oxford University Press, 2007) p. 93.
13. Julian Spilsbury, *The Thin Red Line: An Eyewitness History of the Crimean War* (Weidenfeld & Nicolson, London, 2005) p. 146.
14. Alastair Massie, *op. cit.*, 81.
15. Spilsbury, *op. cit.*, p. 149.
16. Spilsbury, *op. cit.*, pp. 149–50.
17. National Army Museum, 1963-09-5, Recollections of Lieutenant William Forrest, 4th Dragoon Guards.
18. David Buttery, *Messenger of Death, Captain Nolan and the Charge of the Light Brigade* (Pen & Sword, Barnsley, 2008), p. 129.
19. NAM, 07-288-2, Lord Cardigan's Memorandum on the Charge of the Light Brigade.
20. A.W. Kinglake, *The Invasion of the Crimea: Its Origin, and an Account of its Progress Down to the Death of Lord Raglan* (William Blackwood, London, 1877), Vol. IV, p. 282.
21. Geoffrey Moore, *Vincent of the 41st: A Soldier's Battles in the First Afghan and Crimean Wars* (privately published, 1979), p. 37.
22. Kinglake, *op. cit.*, Vol. V, p. 199.
23. Patrick Mercer, *op. cit.*, p. 113.
24. Julian Spilsbury, *op. cit.*, p. 235.
25. Henry Clifford, *Letters and Sketches from the Crimea* (Michael Joseph, London, 1956), p. 93.
26. Julian Spilsbury, *op. cit.*, p. 263.
27. ffrench Blake, *op. cit.*, p. 129.
28. Massie, *op. cit.*, p. 209.
29. Massie, *op. cit.*, p. 225.
30. Quoted in Orlando Figes, *op. cit.*, p. 467.
31. The Royal Collection, RA/VIC/F1/72.
32. Brompton history website: www.bromptonhistory.org.uk
33. Quoted in Orlando Figes, *op. cit.*, p. 467.
34. G.R. Dartnell, D.I.G.H., *A Few Brief Anecdotes Connected With Her Majesty's Visit to the Hospitals at Chatham, 1855–6*.
35. *Ibid.*

Index

Discover Your History

Ancestors • Heritage • Memories

Each issue of *Discover Your History* presents special features and regular articles on a huge variety of topics about our social history and heritage – such as our ancestors, childhood memories, military history, British culinary traditions, transport history, our rural and industrial past, health, houses, fashions, pastimes and leisure ... and much more.

Historic pictures show how we and our ancestors have lived and the changing shape of our towns, villages and landscape in Britain and beyond.

Special tips and links help you discover more about researching family and local history. Spotlights on fascinating museums, history blogs and history societies also offer plenty of scope to become more involved.

Keep up to date with news and events that celebrate our history, and reviews of the latest books and media releases.

Discover Your History presents aspects of the past partly through the eyes and voices of those who were there.

FREE BOOK WHEN YOU SUBSCRIBE TO *Discover Your History*

UK only

Discover Your History is in all good newsagents and also available on subscription for six or twelve issues. For more details on how to take out a subscription and how to choose your free book, call 01778 392013 or visit **www.discoveryourhistory.net**